BY BICYCLE IN IRELAND

BY BICYCLE IN
Ireland

A personal guide to the landscapes
of the Irish Republic

MARTIN RYLE

Impact Books

Blue Stack Mts

L. Neagh

Lower
L. Erne

L. Melvin

L. Gill

L. Allen

Nephin Beg Range

L. Conn

L. Arrow

L. Cullin

L. Key

R. Shannon

L. Mask

L. Ree

Twelve Pins

L. Corrib

Wicklow Mts

L. Derg

Silvermine Mts

R. Barrow

R. Nore

R. Slaney

Blackstairs
Mts

Galtee Mts

R. Suir

Knockmealdowns

Slieve Mish

R. Blackwater

MacGillicuddy's
Reeks

L.
Leane

Derrynasaggart
Mts

R. Lee

First published in Great Britain 1988
by Impact Books, 112 Bolingbroke Grove, London SW11 1DA

British Library Cataloguing in Publication Data
Ryle, Martin
    By bicycle in Ireland : a personal guide
    to the landscapes of the Irish Republic.
    1. Cycling——Ireland——Guide-books
    2. Ireland——Description and travel——1981–
    ——Guide-books
    I. Title
    914.17'04824'0247966   DA980

    ISBN 0–245–54666–9

Acknowledgements
Cover photograph: Lough Conn, County Mayo
(courtesy of Bord Failte/Irish Tourist Board).

Typeset by Photoprint, Torquay, Devon.
Printed by The Guernsey Press, Guernsey.

Contents

Preface

This book is written first of all for cycle-tourists and would-be cycle-tourists. It gives necessary practical information, a picture of the Irish landscape as a whole, and a personal account of twenty-two memorable rides in Ireland. It is not a comprehensive, gazetteer-type guidebook; it is intended to stimulate your imagination, rather than to offer a blueprint or a set itinerary. I hope that it will encourage cyclists to visit Ireland, and prove useful when they are there.

I hope, too, that the book will please a wider circle of readers: armchair travellers interested in the joys and pitfalls of cycling in a lovely, but damp, country; and visitors to Ireland who may have no intention of taking a bicycle, but who would like to share my responses to the landscape, and perhaps to make a note of little-known scenic roads which a motorist, too, might well follow – slowly, I trust, and quietly.

It would give me a lot of pleasure, finally, to think that Irish readers might discover with the help of this book some part of their country which they had not visited before.

I would like to thank Jean-Luc Barbanneau, my publisher, for his enthusiastic support; and to express my gratitude to Peter Cartwright, who drew the maps. Another debt is to everyone at Rayment Cycles in Brighton, where my bicycles have always received expert and friendly help.

My mother, Rosemary Ryle, by looking after Leonie, Jude and Madeleine for long summer weeks over many years, has made it possible for Kate and me to take cycling holidays together, in Ireland and elsewhere: to her, we are both very grateful.

This book is dedicated to Kate Soper, my companion in many of these journeys, and in so much else.

Martin Ryle, 1987

1
CYCLIST'S IRELAND

I first went to Ireland when I was twelve. A school friend, Christy Campbell, invited me to go with him and his parents on their annual visit home. His parents had lived in London for many years. Christy had been born there, but every summer they went back to Ireland, sometimes to the Dublin area and sometimes to the West. We did both, spending a week in the foothills of the Wicklow Mountains before driving in a long arc through Munster (Ireland's southernmost province) to Connemara.

I can remember the justifiable irritation of his parents when Christy and I spent a good part of the journey reading Superman comics in the back of the car. However, the half-seen beauty of that journey, and then the lonely strands and wide skies of Connemara, left a powerful impression which for many years afterwards would revive itself within me, making me say: One day I must go back. Perhaps my ancestry – my mother's father and my father's mother were both Irish – had something to do with this occasional nostalgia, too.

All through my teens and most of my twenties I never did go back. At first I made a student's usual trips, fun at the time although I would not want to repeat them now, hitching down the *autoroutes* and *autostrade* of Mediterranean Europe from city to busy city, and reflecting that it would be pleasant, once in a way, to escape the noise of traffic. Then I began cycling, and my holidays changed forever: the solid villages and wooded farms of Normandy, the stony flower-bedecked towns of the Chianti linked by slippery-surfaced *strade bianche* (white roads), England's Hardy country threaded by lanes and streams – I came to know these and other landscapes as no landscape can be known to the carborne tourist.

Ireland, as I still dimly remembered it, might be a good place to ride, I would say from time to time. It was Kate, though, who first took her bike there, finding in Galway in 1980 the same torrential rain that had kept Thackeray indoors in 1842; but she succeeded in exploring a stretch of the Galway Bay shoreline and inland by

Maam Cross towards the mountains. Then she rode part of the way back east, and her last day she spent cycling high over the Sally Gap in the Wicklows. The variety, beauty and peace of this scenery filled her with enthusiasm, and in 1982, leaving our children in my mother's much appreciated care, we put our bikes on the Irish Mail from Euston to Holyhead and Dun Laoghaire.

Since then I have cycled many times in Ireland, sometimes on my own and sometimes with Kate, and every trip has given me pleasures and memories which have added to my sense of life. I find it hard, now, to contemplate a summer passing in which I do not spend at least a few days on my bicycle in Ireland. As an elderly Anglo-Irish lady, brought up in Cobh when it was called Queenstown and returning still every year to County Cork, told me (with an air of congratulation) in a guesthouse near Ringaskiddy, I am, I suppose, 'hooked': not just by the coasts and loughs and mountains, the green fields and purple bogs, but by the great complex skies, the sweet air washed by rain and renewed by Atlantic winds, scented with flowers and grasses and with the incomparable scent of burning turf, a scent at once light and heavy, sweet and dry. The beauty of Ireland is often austere and touched with melancholy and a sense of mortal transience, shifting suddenly into minor keys as the sunlight fades in clouds, vanishing in mists and rain. For years now this landscape has 'haunted me like a passion'.

You cannot return again and again to a country without moving beyond a response, however intense, to its outward beauty. Through books and newspapers and conversations, I have begun to acquire some sense of Ireland's modern identity and of its geology and geography and history. I have had to reflect on how my Englishness is involved in my feelings about Ireland, and it has become harder for me to ignore the violence in the North, although no tourist in the Republic need confront the 'troubles' directly. Not that I have, as yet, visited Northern Ireland: in this book the word 'Ireland' – the usual conversational term for the Republic as well as the geographical name of the whole island – has as a rule its narrower sense, referring to just twenty-six of the thirty-two counties.

This more developed and in some ways more difficult appreciation of the country cannot cloud the power of its scenery to delight and move. Almost anyone who has been there will tell you how

beautiful Ireland is, and the cyclist is well placed to see that
beauty, travelling slowly enough to absorb the immediate scene
but quickly enough to enjoy the constantly changing panoramas
and perspectives and to note the remarkable variety of the
landscape. Not that you need ride fast or far to know how varied
Ireland is: to drop down from the Silvermines Mountains near
Nenagh into the dairy country of the Tipperary vale, or to cycle
across from the Mayo plains under the rounded shape of Ben
Nephin into the desolate peatbog in the north-west of the county, is
to traverse quite distinct regions in the space of a dozen or two
miles. If I add that there are no extensive areas of industrial
development and very few large towns, that even the classified
roads are for the most part blissfully uncrowded, and that there is
an extensive network of virtually car-free lanes, you will understand that both from an aesthetic and from a practical point of
view Ireland is ideally suited to exploration by bicycle.

The Shape of the Land

Ireland has a tangled geological history, strikingly illustrated on
the coloured map made by the Irish Geological Survey. Even in the
limited area of County Mayo, which you might mistake for a
unified mass of mountain and surrounding moorland, rocks and
deposits of widely separated eras make up the landscape: there
are, to use technical language, 'rocks ranging in age from the
Lewisian gneisses of Erris, through a complex variety of lower
Palaeozoics, to the Carboniferous sediments of Clew Bay, Killala
Bay and the eastern plains' (J B Whittow, *Geology and Scenery in
Ireland*). Any cycle-tourist, without specialist knowledge, will
come to realise, to take another instance, that the sandstone
mountains of the South Country are made of a different stuff from
the quartzite whose glistening conical slopes can be seen in the
peaks of Croagh Patrick in Mayo or Errigal in Donegal.

The plainest contrast is between the extensive limestone of the
central lowlands and the mountains that fringe it on almost every
side, separating the flat midland country from the indented, sea-
worn coastline. Many of the mountains rise well over two thousand
feet, and because in most parts they stand as isolated groups
among surrounding plains, they give a fine impression of blue and
purple height. The cyclist is usually able to find lanes which run

right below the peaks or follow river valleys gradually into their heart without too many long or severe gradients. A friend of mine, a keen cycle-tourist, once asked me, 'But isn't Ireland rather a flat place?' This is far from the case: the rides in chapters 4 and 5 of this book, and especially routes 5, 6, 7 and 8, will take you through unforgettably remote mountain scenery. All the same, it is true that uphill work, in Ireland, is for the most part optional rather than compulsory, and that you might easily contrive a wholly delightful ten days' ride there without once crossing the 400-foot contour.

The cycle-tourist, and indeed any tourist, will be struck not just by the mountains but by the many lakes, most of them astonishingly quiet, and by the long stretches of wild sea-coast. These three elements – mountains, lakes, the sea – are the themes whose innumerable variations make up so much of Ireland's beauty: the later chapters of this book reflect this underlying thematic pattern. There are other features, too, which recur in many regions: glacial deposits, bogs, forests, farmland, and of course towns.

Glacial deposits ('drift') mantle much of the midland plain, but you will notice them as definite landscape features only where the ice has moulded them into the striking shapes of *eskers* and *drumlins*. Both these geological terms are derived from Irish words, and the landforms they denote are particularly visible in Ireland. An esker is a low winding ridge of sandy, gravelly soil, deposited by streams of meltwater that once flowed beneath the ice-sheets. Early settlers used these ridges of firmer ground as routeways across the marshy lowlands, and modern roads still follow them in places. Their modest height means that they do not always appear on the large-scale Ordnance Survey map, whose contours are at 100-foot intervals, but any cyclist crossing the central plain can notice them once she or he knows what to look out for. Near the famous monastic ruin of Clonmacnoise, an esker several miles long forms the Pilgrim's Road along the eastern bank of the Shannon to the crossing at Shannonbridge.

The drumlins, small oval hills aligned in the direction of the ice-flow, lie mainly in a long belt stretching across the northern and western limit of the plain, though there are other local outcrops, most remarkably in Clew Bay where submerged drumlins compose the multitude of tiny islands. The inland drumlin country is hard unrewarding terrain for the farmer, but it has a scenic character and, for me, an intense charm all its own: I try to give some sense of this in my account (route 19) of the wonderful ride up from Lanesborough to Carrick-on-Shannon.

Only when I began to find out about Ireland's geology did I become properly aware of the eskers and the drumlins, but from the start I could hardly miss the bogs. If on your first visit to Ireland you ride west from Dublin, as I did and as many cyclists do, you will come before long to tracts of raised-bog, and will see the insect-like yellow machinery that crawls over its surface harrowing the turf into ridges which are left to dry before being transported to nearby power stations. The blanket-bogs found in the wetter west and on higher ground, which have a different botanical genesis, are not as a rule mechanically exploited (the exception being the great blanket-bog of north-west Mayo): here, and on the smaller raised-bogs too, the turf is cut by hand. Above Ballyporeen opposite the south flank of the Galtee Mountains (see route 2), we talked with a forestry worker who came past our tent in the morning, and he told us how for the price of a licence (I think this cost less than IR£10 per year) he could take all the turf he wanted, which meant an hour or so of work each evening in the summer months. . . . Hereabouts travel writers will tell you that the cut fuel is left in conical stacks to dry out; you may still see such stacks on a mountainside or by a lowland road anywhere. In the rain and wind, you might think, they must reabsorb whatever water evaporates away in sunshine, but since this method has been used for centuries it is presumably effective. Today, however, the stacks are often superseded by plastic fertiliser bags inside which, I suppose, the turf loses its excess moisture while staying sheltered from the rain. This rash of vivid white and yellow plastic is not much in harmony with the subdued, rich colours of the bogs.

Before the end of this century the mechanical harvesting of the bogs will be at an end, the turf exhausted. The resource depletion which elsewhere goes on in the subterranean invisibility of mines and wells is here plain to see on the surface of the land, although it is still hard to believe that these great tracts will so soon run out – and hard to know how Ireland, still heavily dependent on peat for electricity generation, will manage without them.

Economics and energy apart, the bogs have an aesthetic value in the variety they give to the level or gently undulating landscapes of the plain – especially for the cyclist, who has time and fresh air to see and smell the mosses, rough grass, shrubs and thickets which clothe them. In fine weather the edge of a bog is pleasantly dry, springy and solid – a good spot to picnic or make a cup of tea or even put up a tent. Routes 11, 16, 18 and 19 all include rides which are partly, and in the second case almost entirely, over bogland.

In some places, exhausted bogs have been planted with forestry, and forests are widespread on the sides of mountains and on pockets of poor land everywhere. Taking the Republic and the North together, there are well over half a million acres planted, and the area is increasing. It has been argued that entire stretches of the least valuable agricultural land, which no investment can make competitive with better land elsewhere in the EEC, should be afforested, not just for timber but for the recreational potential and rural employment this would give.

These new forests are almost always coniferous. As one element in a varied scene, for instance where they clothe the lower slopes of the Galtees above the hedgerows and meadows of Aherlow (route 3), these dark seas of softwood can be attractive, but most people agree that they are monotonous when they stretch endlessly across mountain, hill and plain. This is rare in Ireland, the plantations being limited in size. You may ride for ten or twenty minutes through state forests, enjoying their scent and their coolness (or the shelter they provide from rain), stopping maybe at one of the simple picnic clearings made by the Forest and Wildlife Service, but you will not spend so long in them that you get weary of their uniform colouring or frustrated at the way they obscure the view.

Deciduous woodland is rare in Ireland, which has suffered severe and systematic deforestation since early colonial days and is now one of the least wooded countries in Europe. The best trees were taken for the British navy, the oakwoods around Lough Derg (on the lower Shannon) and elsewhere were used for iron-smelting charcoal, and in later times the hard-pressed Irish population, refused access to what remained of the landlords' trees, stripped and felled most of the remaining unenclosed woodland. You will see extensive deciduous woods along the seaward foothills of Wicklow; further west, around Killarney and along the west Cork headlands (see routes 14 and 15), you will ride through brief but luxuriantly leafy stretches of wood, too. Elsewhere the treelessness of Ireland is not always evident, either, for there are splendid hedgerows in parts of the central plain and in much of Tipperary and Limerick. Some former landed estates, such as Rockingham House (see route 20), possessed fine woods which survive to this day: here too, in the richly timbered country running around Lough Key and the foot of Lough Arrow, you would take Ireland for a well-wooded land. However, ancient forest survives only in a few isolated patches: we were told by a young man on a motorbike, who stopped and sat with us by our fire when we were camping near Lough Gill in County Sligo, that nearby Slish Wood or Sleuth Wood (mentioned by Yeats) was such an ancient oakwood fragment, inaccessible by road and difficult to enter even for a walker.

Most of Ireland is farmed. The character of the farming changes markedly as the soil quality declines from east to west across the country. In the south-east and in the eastern part of the midland plain there is a fair amount of arable farming, but pasture and hay predominate everywhere else. West of the Shannon the grazing is poorer, there is more unenclosed land, and the mountains give the scenery a wilder feel, as they do in the country south of Slieve Bloom. Mountainsides are grazed, often as unenclosed common: crossing the 1,000-foot Healy Pass on the Beara Peninsula, west Cork, you will see black-faced sheep munching stolidly in the mist, and in the remotest country you may ride past cows browsing on a lane-verge or a bog. Camping in the Pullans in south County Donegal (route 10), we watched a small herd of cattle work their way across the peat and rough grass in front of our tent, and the youngest of the herd watched us too, breaking off his near-perpetual feeding to pay us full attention. He must have been struck by what he saw – maybe this was his first sighting of a bicycle – for he kicked his heels in the air and made excited dashes and sallies across the tussocks. These cows were the only living sign that evening of a nearby human presence, for not a car or a walker passed on the lane above us.

Solitude and silence are yours if you look for them in Ireland, but you will usually see a scattering of farms and cottages even in the wildest view. Ireland has a very low density of population but that population is rather evenly distributed, apart from the concentration in and around Dublin. Clustered villages are rare: cottages, often newly-built bungalows, are spread along the roads. Aesthetically it is easy to criticise these, for their 'Spanish arches' and general air of ostentation are not in harmony with our ideas of what is rustically traditional, but in many cases these new buildings will be a welcome escape from an overcrowded two-room cottage – itself perhaps the successor to a wretched nineteenth-century cabin. On most lanes you will pass a mile of hedge or field for every group of buildings that you see, and the country feels peopled, inhabited (this is after all an overwhelmingly agricultural economy), rather than crowded. The population density of the Irish Republic is about 45 people per square km: in the UK, the figure is 230 per square km.

The even spread of rural population has practical advantages for the cycle-tourist, since it means that village stores and market towns are well distributed. Outside the remotest parts – north Mayo, Donegal, west Cork – you will almost always be within an hour's ride of basic provisions (I say more about this in chapter 2).

Large towns hardly exist. Dublin, Cork, Limerick and Waterford are the biggest, although of these only the first two are large by British standards. Galway illustrates the small population even of important regional towns, for it is the undoubted if unofficial 'capital of Connacht', with its own university, yet it numbers only around 30,000 people. Sligo has just half that many, and Donegal town, with just a couple of thousand inhabitants, is not much more than a village by the standards of south-east Britain.

Guidebooks often declare that Ireland's towns are undistinguished, singling out the same few places – Westport, Clonmel – as exceptions to the rule. It is true that centuries of absentee landlordism and colonial exploitation, together perhaps with the lack of good-quality local building stone, have given most Irish towns a modest and sometimes cramped feel, and that they are not often laid out in any imaginative plan. They are sometimes made scruffy by litter: 'litter and the indiscriminate dumping of rubbish and waste materials are a particular problem, common to town and country, and marked enough to merit attention in any survey of the Irish landscape', as the geographer F Aalen notes with academic dryness and accuracy in *Man and the Landscape in Ireland*. (I should add that attempts, not notably successful, are being made to change this, and that while on country lanes litter is rare, you will occasionally notice it beside classified roads.) But this one-dimensional response to Irish towns, with its implication that their main duty is to look nice, misses other qualities that they do possess: their liveliness, their rootedness in an immediate hinterland. They have an appropriate scale and an integration with their surroundings which reminds one of the market towns of rural France rather than of the mushrooming dormitory settlements of south-east Britain. Tobercurry and Templemore, Tullamore and Clonakilty: I have happy memories of these and many other 'undistinguished' towns in Ireland, as well as of places such as Carrick-on-Shannon and Manorhamilton in County Leitrim or Bunclody on the Carlow/Wexford border, places which are more than thriving market centres, for they have superb natural settings beside rivers or in the shadow of the mountains.

The Regions of Ireland

This book does not have the region-by-region format usual in travel guides. I have wanted to approach the landscape in a way that will bring out its variety and its underlying unity, and I have also wanted to avoid suggesting that this is a comprehensive guide. It is not; it is personal, and I have cycled every route I describe. Inevitably, then, some regions receive fuller coverage than others.

I have already said that the North is not included, and I have not travelled, either, in the more easterly border counties (Louth, Monaghan, Cavan) of the Republic. These are the main omissions. There are other areas – the south-east corner of the country, Wicklow, Clare, the midlands – which do not feature in the routes described even though they are attractive to the cyclist. To compensate for these latter gaps in the record, and to give a fuller picture of the landscapes you will meet in different parts of Ireland, I now give a brief sketch of the main regions, with the needs and preferences of cyclists especially in mind.

Wicklow and the Leinster Mountains (*Route 1*)

The Wicklow Mountains rise directly from the sea just south of Dublin, making Dun Laoghaire the most attractive of all the Irish ferry ports. Thanks to their closeness to the capital they are ideal cycling country for the visitor who has only a few days and wants to see something of the country's cultural life as well as of its landscape. They make a convenient touring area, too, if you wish to travel light and hire a bicycle when you arrive.

However, this is strenuous country, untypical of Ireland, a solid block of high ground with few river valleys running into it: 'In the Wicklows . . . the mountains form a true massif where the 1,000-foot contour encloses an area of more than 200 square miles' (J B Whittow, *Geology and Scenery in Ireland*). The upper slopes are moorland, with little shelter from wind and rain: if the clouds come down, as they did when we were there, you will find it less daunting to skirt their seaward flank on the roads and lanes that run south from Dublin and Bray. The flattest and most sheltered route is on the main Dublin–Wexford road on the narrow coastal plain, but I would imagine this can be rather busy. We took quiet lanes running parallel to classified roads through Roundwood and Laragh to Rathdrum.

South of the main Wicklow mass, the granite runs on in the impressive, narrow chain of the Blackstairs Mountains which mark the border between Wexford and Carlow and whose highest peak, Mount Leinster, can be seen far across the rolling land of north-east Munster.

Route 1 crosses the Blackstairs ridge at its lowest point, the Scullogue Gap south of Bunclody, taking you through an attractive col from the Leinster massif into the river-valleys, plains and mountains of the South Country.

The South Country (*Routes 2, 3, 4 and 18*)

Geologists call this the 'ridge and valley province', and it has a marked east-west grain, with the Suir and Blackwater rivers running between the abrupt, high mountains of the Knockmealdowns and the Comeragh and Monavullagh ranges south of Clonmel, and the Galtees south of Tipperary town.

The cyclist can follow the rivers, where a classified road on one bank is often paralleled by a lane on the other. The Blackwater near Lismore runs through a particularly beautiful pastoral valley, richly wooded and peaceful, with Lismore Castle superbly sited on the south bank. Lanes follow smaller rivers and streams into many of the mountains, although the Galtees, too imperiously steep for road or wheel, will have to be admired from afar unless you leave your bicycle for a day and climb on foot to the summit of Galtymore – at 3,018 feet, Ireland's highest inland peak.

All this is rich grazing land, with the big creamery at Mitchelstown producing excellent butter and cheese. The contrast between green plain and sheer mountain gives this region its character, as memorable as the wilder and more celebrated scenery further to the west. When we set off for west Cork and Kerry, riding through the Blackstairs and over by Clonmel and Millstreet in the wet August of 1985, we were enchanted by this middle stretch of the journey. The Galtees, above all, are unforgettable, their long ridge rising like a fin from the rolling sea of grassland and lower hills. You will see that unmistakable ridge from innumerable vantages: from the low downland north-east of Cork city, where it shares the horizon with the peaks of west Waterford; from the foothills of the Derrynasaggart range as you freewheel down into the wide valley of the upper Blackwater; from Slievenamuck above Aherlow and from the Kilworth Hills by Mitchelstown; from the Tipperary Vale and from the flat land of east County Limerick, where we sat in a meadow hedged with tall hazel trees, warming ourselves at our campfire after a cool showery day and talking with the farmer, gazing now at the line of ragged cloud drawn by the wind across the last glow of sunset, and now at the distant Galtees rising darkly into the pale stars of the south-eastern sky.

To the north-west, the South Country ends at the Silvermines Hills and the lower stretches of Lough Derg, largest of the Shannon lakes and the limit of navigable water before the river passes through the gorge of Killaloe and the hydroelectric station of Ardnacrusha by Limerick city to the sea.

Routes 2 and 3 cross valleys and pastures, mostly lowland riding, but with short, stiff climbs taking you onto ridges with fine views. *Route 4* follows a river high into the empty Silvermines, as quiet a place as you will find in inland Ireland. *Route 18* runs for miles along the western shore of Lough Derg.

Cork and Kerry *(Routes 5, 6, 12, 13, 14 and 15)*

Here is some of Ireland's best-known scenery. Beyond the quieter charms of the south coast lie the headlands and peninsulas of west Cork and Kerry, and just inland are the Killarney lakes and MacGillicuddy's Reeks, with Carrauntoohil (3,414 feet) the highest mountain in the country. All along the indented seaboard, high mountains plunge into Atlantic bays, placid on a blue day but harsh and gloomy when the sky darkens and the west wind gets up. This can be wild country and if you avoid the busiest places it can be remote too, but it is softened by the mildness of the climate, often damp but seldom cold, and by the luxuriance of the vegetation. Even the steepest and highest slopes seem clothed in vivid grass, there are often blooms of fuchsia on either side of the lanes, and the woods have a leafy rankness that can seem sinister if you ride beneath their mossy shade after a long stretch of open, rocky seashore.

Further inland, cyclists who want to explore less celebrated scenery will be amply rewarded if they climb into the empty uplands of the Derrynasaggart and Boggeragh Mountains.

In the summer months, there will be traffic on the classified roads, and my routes steer clear of the touristic circuits (Killarney, the Ring of Kerry, the Dingle Peninsula). I avoid, too, the plain of north Kerry around Tralee, where the piecemeal development is unworthy of the country it threatens to spoil. But most of Cork and Kerry is undeveloped and uncrowded by British and Continental standards, and as you ride out along Sheep's Head or the Beara you come to a landscape as unspoiled as you could wish. The motorists hereabouts, like their counterparts elsewhere, seemingly lack the wits or the maps – long may the lack continue – to turn off down the lanes, so you need only pick your route with some thought to find quiet riding through country that deserves all the praise it has received since Thackeray wrote in his *Irish Sketchbook* that 'the journey from Glengarriff to Kenmare is one of astonishing beauty. . . . Rock, wood, and sea stretch around the traveller – a thousand delightful pictures'.

From a practical point of view, you should bear in mind when planning your trip that any one of the headlands is a day's ride, often more, by the time you have cycled out and back. If you want to explore this region thoroughly and have a limited time in which to do so, you will need either to take a train or bus over from the east coast, or to catch the ferry (if the service is still operating) from Swansea to Cork harbour.

Route 5 starts at Kenmare on the sea, and takes you up by gentle gradients over the 1,000-foot contour and into the high ground of the Derrynasaggart range. *Route 6* runs from near Killarney out along the Kenmare River and by empty lanes up to the Ballagh-beama Gap in the seaward flank of MacGillicuddy's Reeks.

Route 12 follows the south Cork coast through Kinsale and on westwards by way of charmingly quiet yachting harbours and wooded creeks. *Routes 13, 14 and 15* run along the shores and over the rocky spines of the three southernmost Atlantic headlands: Mizen Head, Sheep's Head, and the Beara Peninsula.

The Burren

I have not yet managed to explore by bicycle the strange limestone plateau of the Burren, an extensive area of north County Clare famous for its geological and botanical curiosities. I have passed through in a van, and can agree with all those who praise this unparalleled landscape, where white rock breaks the ground and the small, stony fields stretch across a treeless expanse except where thickets cluster in hollows or a patch of thorn grows along one of the low ridges.

At the Atlantic, the plateau culminates in the Cliffs of Moher, and along its northern and north-western coast you will look across Galway Bay to the three Aran Islands, geologically an extension of the Burren. Alluring or daunting depending on the weather, these islands will always seem challenging in their remoteness at the edge of the open Atlantic.

Since I have not cycled there, I give no routes for the Burren. You might visit it by travelling south round the head of Galway Bay after touring Connemara and Mayo, or you might come north from Kerry by way of the Shannon ferry from Tarbert to Killimer. Or you might come by way of Lough Derg – from Scarriff or Mount-shannon, say, on the south-west shore of that lovely lake (see route 18). On lanes by Lough Graney and Lough Cutra, you would pass westwards through Gort. It was from the forge at Gort that the ironwork came for the restoration of Thoor Ballylee, where Yeats lived briefly and which is now open as a museum. Lady Gregory's estate at Coole Park was near here too, but the house no longer stands, pulled down in the 1940s for the mere value of the building materials. 'No words of condemnation,' as Sean Jennett writes in his guide to *Connacht*, 'are enough for the idiots who allowed this to happen, and no denunciation is too hard for the yahoo who knocked down the house of Coole. . . . It should have been a shrine of the Irish literary renaissance.'

This whole area, including the Burren itself, is almost as much Yeats country as the Sligo district. It is much mirrored in his later and more direct poetry – his sterner poetry, you might say, recalling what he wrote in memory of Major Robert Gregory:

> We dreamed that a great painter had been born
> To cold Clare rock and Galway rock and thorn
> To that stern colour and that delicate line . . .

It is cold sternness rather than delicacy that I remember from the Burren, but I must go back and discover it again.

Mayo and Connemara (*Routes 7, 8, 11, 16 and 22*)

Connemara is the empty Atlantic region that lies between Galway Bay and the deep fjord of Killary Harbour. Similar terrain continues north of Killary to Clew Bay, and this district, properly called Murrisk, is often included in the term 'Connemara'. There are striking mountains separated by deep valleys, numberless lochans (small lakes), and an indented, ice-scrubbed coastline (the ice was glacial and the region now has a mild, wet climate), with rocky and sandy coves and small farms clinging to the strip of lowland between the mountains and the sea.

Even in fine weather it is an austere place, though an extremely beautiful one. When cloud comes down it grows desolate and gloomy, with sea and sky and mountains all lost to sight and the varied colours merged in one purplish grey. At times like this I recall Flann O'Brien's savage novel *The Poor Mouth*, written in Irish and translated by Patrick Power: O'Brien's Corkadoragh is a quintessence of every rain-stricken, sea-smitten hamlet all down Ireland's west coast, and his evocation of rain and storm seems especially appropriate to Connemara:

> The night before I was born, it happened that my father and Martin O'Bannassa were sitting on top of the hen-house, gazing at the sky to judge the weather and also chatting honestly and quietly about the difficulties of life.
>
> Well, now, Martin, said my father, the wind is from the north and there's a forbidding look about the White Bens; before the morning there'll be rain and we'll get a dirty tempestuous night of it that will knock a shake out of us even if we're in the very bed. And look here! Martin, isn't it the bad sign that the ducks are in the nettles?

In Connemara, as anywhere on Ireland's west coast, foul or fair weather can give way with extraordinary suddenness to their opposite. Do not despair if your first day is wet. To get the true flavour of the place, you will want to see it under more than one sky.

Connemara lies partly in County Galway and partly in County Mayo. Mayo is large and diverse, and includes much fine cycling country. The rolling eastern plain is sometimes dismissed by motorists as uninteresting, but cyclists will appreciate its almost somnolent peace and the contrast between its pastures, stone-walled but often wooded, and the barer, wilder terrain to the west.

The plain is divided from Connemara by Lough Mask, my own favourite of all Ireland's lakes – or rather, of those that I have seen, for Mayo alone has a dozen loughs a mile or more in length, and any number of smaller waters. North beyond Westport lie the peninsula and island of Corraun and Achill, their heights continued inland in the Nephin Beg range and then in the tallest peak, Ben Nephin, standing apart from the lower tops and looking down over Lough Conn and Lough Cullin. North Mayo has a little-visited coastline of wild cliffs. In the north-west there is that great blanket-bog, and on the far side of it the remote Mullet and Erris Peninsula beyond Belmullet.

Route 7 brings out the variety of Connemara: two mountain cols, the shores of a broad lough and of three smaller mountain ones, and at Killary Harbour a glimpse of the Atlantic. *Route 8* follows an unmetalled forest road through the deserted heart of the Nephin Beg.

Route 11 lies mostly in County Sligo, but ends near Lough Cullin in Mayo. *Route 16* crosses the peatbog of north-west Mayo, an austere and even gloomy ride, in contrast to the sheer delight of *route 22*, which runs for a dozen miles between the Connemara mountains and the shining waters of Lough Mask.

Donegal and North Sligo (*Routes 9, 10 and 17*)

County Donegal is both rugged and remote. There is scope here for a week and more on your bicycle, but if you want to see all of Donegal you will be well advised to take a train or a bus a good part of the way over from the east: from Dublin to the Donegal border is four or five days' ride. You must hope for fair weather, too, for the mountain ridges which run from north-east to south-west across almost the entire interior of the county are inhospitable, not to mention invisible, when cloud comes down.

We saw only the southern part of Donegal, but we saw enough to appreciate both the wildness of the empty inland ranges and the unspoiled beauty of the coast. There are winding inlets and sea-loughs in the north, miles of sandy beaches in the west, and impressive sheer cliffs in the Slieve League headland running out to Glencolumbkille. Roads, though not many of them, strike north-east along the valleys from the more populous coastal strip. The most southerly of these, from Donegal town to Ballybofey and Stranorlar, is the busiest: further north are lanes and minor roads which must surely offer some of the loneliest cycling in Ireland. This is one area where you should be sure to carry iron rations and to watch the mechanical condition of your bicycle, for you will often find yourself a long way from any sizeable settlement.

North of Sligo town the landscape is dominated by the curious flat-topped limestone ridge that culminates in Ben Bulben, separating the wide bays of Sligo and Donegal. The ride under Ben Bulben, so long as you have sense enough to pick your way along the quiet lanes, is delightful, and the Pullans in south Donegal, just through the narrow corridor which hereabouts connects Donegal to the rest of the Irish Republic, are fine, unpopulated country.

You may be puzzled to see County Donegal referred to as part of Ulster. 'Ulster' is sometimes used as a synonym for 'Northern Ireland', but properly speaking it denotes the northern province of Ireland according to the traditional fourfold division (with Connacht in the west, Leinster in the east, and Munster in the south). Ulster in this usage includes Donegal, Monaghan and Cavan in the Republic, as well as the six counties belonging to the United Kingdom.

Route 9 runs along lanes from Sligo under Ben Bulben to Ballyshannon, where the Erne river meets the Atlantic. *Route 10* takes you from Donegal town to Lough Eske below the Blue Stacks Mountains, and so southwards to the lakes and moorland of the Pullans. *Route 17* explores the Slieve League Peninsula – the sandy beaches of the north shore of Donegal Bay, the bogs of the moun-tainous interior, the extraordinarily quiet dunes and crags and streamlets of Loughros Beg Bay near Maghera, and the busy fishing port of Killybegs.

South Sligo and the Shannon above Athlone (*Routes 11, 19, 20 and 21*)

Sligo is separated from Mayo by the long ridge of the Ox

Mountains, and to their east lies a stretch of rolling limestone country, an extension of the great midland plain – pleasant riding, with alternating bogs and pastures. South-east Sligo is hillier, even if 'mountains' is a grandiose appellation for the Curlew and Bricklieve ranges, neither of which rises much over 1,000 feet. Beyond the Bricklieves and Curlews, and partly in County Roscommon, are the wooded waters of Lough Key and Lough Arrow, and north of them a fine river-threaded drumlin country. Towards Sligo town is Lough Gill, where you can make the two-minute trip by rowing boat to Yeats' Lake Isle of Innisfree; and north and west of here you are in Leitrim, a remote and sparsely inhabited county with bald uplands, narrow valleys, and many lakes both large and small.

From Lough Key, the Boyle River flows east to join the Shannon just above Carrick. North and south of Carrick-on-Shannon is a most lovely landscape, a combination of river and lake and rushy meadow and rounded drumlin hills whose inland spaciousness seems 'made quiet by the power / Of harmony, and the deep power of joy', to quote Wordsworth's *Tintern Abbey*. Downstream the Shannon broadens into Lough Ree, with an extent of bog undulating away into Roscommon on its western shores, and on the east the hedgerows and rolling fields of Longford merging into the central plain below Athlone.

This is mostly easy cycling, and scenic cycling too. If Atlantic winds are bringing the rain in over the seacoasts, you will find more sheltered riding here, but it is very much deserving of a visit in its own right, and not just as an alternative to the better-known attractions of the west.

Route 11 heads west into County Mayo across the limestone country around Tubbercurry, with the Ox Mountains on the horizon most of the way and occasional views (in clear weather) of the distant mountains of Connemara. *Route 19* and *route 20* explore Loughs Ree, Key and Arrow and the lowland country of the Shannon valley near Carrick. *Route 21* lies mostly in Leitrim, taking you alongside Lough Melvin on the Fermanagh frontier and down by slaty, mountain-girt Manorhamilton to Lough Gill.

The Central Plain

If you ride more or less due west from Dublin to Galway, perhaps following the Grand Canal for the first two-thirds of your journey, you will have around you all the way landscapes of the central plain: flat or gently rolling fields, sometimes with hedgerows winding between them, alternating with raised-bogs and drained by streams and rivers that make their way sluggishly but inevitably to the Shannon. West of the Shannon the ground grows stonier and you feel the impending power of the Atlantic and its gales, but the continuity of the plain, which barely rises above 300 feet, is not broken until you see the granite moorlands and quartzite peaks of Connemara.

This is cattle country for the most part, producing meat in great quantities, as you will see from the stockyards and butchers' shops of towns like Ballyhaunis or Tullamore. Scenically, it lacks the drama of the celebrated touristic regions, and Bord Failte (the Irish Tourist Board) is trying to upgrade its image by encouraging people to drop the old name 'the midlands' and to replace it with 'the lakelands' – which may be fitting for parts of Longford, Roscommon and Westmeath, but is hardly applicable to Offaly, Kildare or east Galway. I prefer to take the midlands as they are, workaday perhaps, a place that you pass through on your way somewhere else (which is why this region barely figures in my routes), but a pleasant place to pass through, certainly for the cyclist. Cyclists used to English levels of road traffic and population density will delight in the sheer spacious calm of the plain. After crossing London, perhaps, on the way to Euston and Holyhead, after a tiring journey and then the bustle of Dublin at breakfast time, your holiday begins – you can feel it beginning – as you turn down some midland lane or minor road: you are in another country.

The flatness of the midlands makes for easy going and if you are in the mood for a big day's mileage this is ideal terrain, especially heading back east with the wind in your tail. In the landscape, too, flatness has its charms: when you do climb a low ridge or hill (perhaps an esker), you have long vistas of pastoral country. And the wide sky stretches away to the far horizon on every side.

History, Politics

Cycling in Ireland, you are bound to pass ecclesiastical and military ruins, not for the most part as spacious or as well restored as the best known British examples, but often compensating for this by the unspoiled rural or urban environment in which they stand. There are many memorials of an older, preliterate culture: you may see in some otherwise unremarkable field, as I saw when I rode up the east side of the Laney valley above Macroom in County Cork, a group of stones standing where early Irish settlers erected them four thousand years and more ago. Since almost the whole surface of the land has been used for grazing or cultivation of some sort, Frank Mitchell, in the Preface to his fascinating book, *The Irish Landscape*, goes so far as to say that 'no matter where we stand and look about us [in Ireland], we cannot see any area, large or small, high or low, that has not been altered . . . by man's activities.'

Ireland's history is in many ways exceptional: the Romans never ventured there, Gaelic language and culture survived into the nineteenth century. It is also complicated and, in its recent and contemporary phase, bitterly controversial. It would be absurd to offer a summary of it here and I do not intend to do so, although in my route descriptions I do occasionally refer to some monument or some piece of local history directly connected with the country through which the road passes.

It would be equally absurd for me to give my views in a few paragraphs on Partition and the future of Northern Ireland: I have tried honestly to record my feelings and thoughts on the occasions when I have found myself impelled by the surrounding country or townscape to reflect on these themes, but even if those reflections had crystallised (which they have not) into a coherent 'opinion', I do not regard myself as qualified to put that forward in public.

However, people thinking of visiting southern Ireland – British people in particular – will naturally want to know how far, if at all, their travels there are likely to confront them with echoes of the 'Troubles' in the North. It should be said at once that so far as your personal safety goes, there is no reason whatever to feel apprehensive: paradoxical as it may sound, the Irish Republic is an extraordinarily peaceful place to be. The proverbial friendliness of its people is extended without reserve to British as to other tourists. Only once in seven holidays have I felt any shadow of hostility directed towards my Englishness, and even on that occasion, in Ardara in County Donegal, I think my slight unease may well have been paranoid imagining rather than justified response.

If you cycle in the frontier counties (I have not cycled in Louth, Monaghan or Cavan, but I have spent time in Leitrim and Donegal, and also in Sligo, which is virtually 'border country'), you will see BRITS OUT, usually in faded paint, on walls and road surfaces, and there will be Sinn Fein posters on lamp-posts here and there. Nowhere in the Republic does more than a very small minority support the Provos – support for constitutional nationalism and solidarity with Northern Catholics are of course another matter – but that minority is slightly less small along the border. If you prefer not to confront the evidence of this, you need only keep a little to the south. In *A Place Apart*, which I would urge you to read if you do want to find out more about the North, Dervla Murphy writes that 'south of the Dublin–Galway line there is little sense of personal involvement with Northern Ireland; it seems much further away than Britain, where so many people have lived and worked, or even than the USA.'

Let me conclude these unhappy but necessary remarks by repeating that you can travel throughout the Republic in complete safety. The welcome you will receive, the long and friendly conversations you are sure to have with Irish people, will add breadth and depth to your appreciation of Ireland's natural beauty.

'Politics', in an Irish context, immediately suggests the North, but there are many other issues on the Republic's agenda nowadays. What will become of Ireland's long-standing military non-alignment as the country is drawn more closely into a European Community all of whose other members are also members of NATO? Can Ireland find an energy strategy and a type of 'modernisation' which preserves its unspoiled landscape, is compatible with its still fundamentally rural pattern of life, and provides a better living for the marginal farmers of the west and more employment opportunities for the young people who are once again emigrating in large numbers? Ireland's 'modern' or 'European' identity is in many ways simply a reflection of Western European capitalism; it cohabits uncomfortably with a 'traditional' culture or ideology (part authentic tradition, part nationalist revival) which itself seems to an outsider to be an unlikely blend of Catholicism, Gaelic sports, the Irish language, and an unfinished – perhaps unfinishable – project of national unity. Neither this contradictory culture nor the kind of life you might lead in

Ireland's small towns is readily compatible with the modern, metropolitan image of 'success': how will these contradictions work themselves out, and can Ireland, as one country or as two, preserve or recreate a distinct national identity for the next century?

I have no special ability to discuss these questions, but I have reflected on them in passing when I have seen or heard something in the course of my cycling that has made me aware of them.

The Weather and Other Hazards

> A moon as round and bright as any moon that ever shone, and riding in a sky perfectly cloudless, gave us good promise of a fine day for the morrow, which was to be devoted to the lakes in the neighbourhood of Ballinahinch. . . . But no man can speculate on Irish weather. I have seen a day beginning with torrents of rain that looked as if a deluge was at hand, clear up in a few minutes. . . . So in like manner, after the astonishingly fine night, there came a villainous dark day.

This is Thackeray writing of his visit to Connemara during his tour of 1842. Anyone who travels in Ireland will agree that its weather is changeable and often wet – hardly surprising given the country's exposed maritime position in the track of successive Atlantic depressions.

Let us not exaggerate and misrepresent Irish rain. We were in Ireland in August 1985 and in August 1986, both record-breakingly wet months, but were able to camp out comfortably on all but five of a combined total of eighteen nights. In 1987, we had some memorably wild and wet mornings, and a couple of long damp days when the cloud just would not lift from the mountains and headlands of Donegal; but there was only one wet evening out of fourteen. Besides, although you might think a cyclist is particularly vulnerable to bad weather, that is not my own view. Stuck inside a car, I am depressed by the merest drizzle, listening disconsolately to the windscreen-wipers, thinking: Nothing to be done until this rain stops. Out on my bicycle, I simply get on with my holiday. Of course I look forward to bright skies and better visibility, but nowadays I can truly say that I have learned to ride with pleasure through the rain, once I have taken – almost literally, some Irish mornings – the plunge.

In Ireland, as in Britain, the cycle-tourist must expect some wet weather and make due practical preparation. Properly waterproof clothing is invaluable: I say more about this in chapter 2. If you are taking a tent, allow enough spare cash for occasional nights in a Bed and Breakfast: the rain often eases off towards evening, but by then, after hours splashing through puddles, the prospect of a hot shower and a dry bed may be irresistible – especially if your sleeping bag is wet, as *can* happen however carefully you thought you had protected it. . . .

Mental and psychological preparations can be made, too. My own policy as regards weather forecasts is simple: when it is wet, I buy a paper and look hopefully at the weather-chart, but when it is dry I leave well alone (the forecast is not very dependable, and is often hedged about with evasions and regional variations). Bear in mind that wet mornings really do very often turn into blue afternoons, and that successive wet days, although not unheard of, are rare: here, the rapid changeableness of the climate is on your side.

Above all, look forward in a positive spirit to what Irish weather has to offer. Don't set your heart on hot sun and blue sky, and call nothing else 'good weather'. Clear skies at dawn and dusk you may well see in Ireland, but during the day some cloud will almost invariably build up, as the sun warms the humid air: this is by no means necessarily a mark of impending rain, and the cloud often thins out and disappears towards evening. The Irish climate may frustrate you or madden you at times, but it brings its own unparalleled gifts – a quality of light unforgettable in its clouded shifts and changes, its softness in most conditions and its sudden brilliant clarity under a dry wind and a bright sun; its complicated cloudscapes, which can achieve astonishing beauty at sunset after rain; temperatures hardly ever too warm or too cool for comfortable cycling at any time from May to September; and long summer evenings, with the light out in the west on a June or July night lingering in the sky or above the sea until after eleven on the clock. Rain apart, the other potential weather hazard is wind, which can be strong and persistent, especially in the west. In summer, fortunately, the wetter days tend to be the stiller ones; the northwest wind, often strong, is usually dry. But when planning your itinerary and your timetable, you should make some allowance for the likelihood of winds from a generally western quarter.

The natural environment in Ireland is in most other respects kind. Cyclists will rejoice to know that the motorist, potentially the deadliest of species, is easily avoided and generally of a placid and friendly disposition when you do encounter her or him. Midges can be irritating if you are camping: I have been tormented by them a couple of times, in Kerry and Cork, although further north they have never bothered me much. The rule here is to avoid streams and pools in still weather: a breeze is enough to keep the midges away. I have however camped right beside lakes in Mayo and found them no more than a slight irritant even on windless evenings.

There are no snakes in Ireland, a fact for which I am deeply and no doubt irrationally grateful.

Dogs will bark fiercely as you ride down quiet lanes; they may dash out and run alongside you, yelping, until you are clear of what they regard as their stretch of road. Remember that if you freak out and fall off, you could hurt yourself: don't let the dogs alarm you (a stupid little cur did once bite my ankle, in County Tipperary, but no dangerous animal will be left unchained). My policy, based on long experience of dogs Irish, British, Italian and French, is to slow down, look the animal in the eye, and speak to it firmly but gently – whatever your true feelings about the hound in question.

2
READY TO GO

This book is aimed primarily at cycle-tourists. You can of course cycle in Ireland without embarking on a full-blown tour. Bicycles are available for hire in many towns: Bord Failte produce a guide with relevant details. You can also take bikes with you on the roof of a car, or on the back of a camper van or 'recreation vehicle': I remember seeing a West German *Wohnwagen* embarking on the Swansea–Cork ferry, the four bicycles of its inmates dangling like bracelets from the back of the enormous truck. Hiring bikes or taking them by car makes sense if you have young children with you, or if you doubt whether you are fit enough or bold enough to load everything you need onto your machine. However, once you have tried it, and assuming you *are* reasonably fit, you will agree that cycling is such a pleasant way of getting about that it is a pity to find yourself reliant on any other mode of transport. You are restricted, too, if you have not come on your own bike, insofar as you will have to return to your car or van or to the shop where you hired your cycle. The routes in this book are not round trips: in this respect, and in much of what I say in the present chapter, I have in mind the cycle-tourist rather than the holiday-maker who has chosen to take a bicycle along.

A cycle-tour is, I suppose, an adventurous kind of holiday. You depend on your own legs to get you from place to place, you are committed to spending the days under the open sky, and you must be able to keep your mount in running order. This adventurousness is part of the attraction: it is odd that, while the truly dangerous (and to my mind unpleasurable) feats of transatlantic balloonists, solitary rowers and Amazon explorers attract so much publicity and admiration, most of us seem incapable, on our own travels, of breaking away from our dependence on the internal combustion engine (with its noise and pollution, which do nothing to preserve the environments we choose for our vacations).

You do need to be, or to become, resourceful and independent-spirited to make the most of a cycle tour. But it is a mistake to think that cycle touring is perilous, or that it demands a high degree of fitness and mechanical expertise. It is a mistake, too, to imagine that cycle-tourists are necessarily bicycle freaks, obsessed with their machines and the accessories and accoutrements that go with them.

I began touring in a state of considerable innocence. My bike was unsuitable: the only real racing machine I have ever owned, a lovely Holdsworth with a short wheel-base, no mudguards, and puncture-prone one-piece tubular tyres. It was also considerably too small for me. For all that, it served me well for years: it was on my Holdsworth, lovingly (if incompetently) repainted in brilliant yellow, that I first rode into the Irish countryside. I did make avoidable mistakes in those early days, and I would have been well advised to seek some knowledgeable guidance, but I don't want to give you the idea that there is anything terribly daunting or demanding involved in taking a holiday on your bicycle.

Fitness

Compared to riding about in a car, cycling is energetic. It would be silly to set off on a cycle tour unless you are already in the habit of cycling regularly (apart from the fitness aspect, you will want to be using your machine to be sure that it is in good running order). But once you have got accustomed to riding even a few miles each week, and to carrying some weight on your bike – a week's shopping will do fine – you should find that you adapt without much difficulty to the rhythm of a tour. I ride no more than twenty or thirty miles a week most of the year, but on holiday I find no problem in covering fifty or sixty miles every day.

Not that 'fifty or sixty miles', or any other distance, represents some kind of target that you should set yourself. It is easy to spoil your holiday by setting barely achievable 'goals' for each day's riding. What is the point in pressing on through the discomfort barrier, and ending the day tired and dispirited rather than pleasantly relaxed? You will soon discover what kind of daily mileage – it could be anything from twenty to seventy miles – you can cover with ease. Once you have established this, plan the itinerary to fit in with your known abilities and preferences, instead of stretching yourself to fit in with some arbitrary schedule.

Ireland is kind to the cyclist who lacks an athlete's physical condition, as I most certainly do. Compared with upland Wales, the West Country, or the hills of Normandy or Tuscany, it is undemanding country. The lowlands and river valleys are easy going, and, as I have said, you will often find flattish lanes running close to the mountains, too. If you do want to climb over high cols, there are opportunities to do so, and superb views to be had as a reward; but even here, Ireland is considerate of your legs and lungs, for there are plenty of long, gradual ascents that will take you to several hundred feet by easy stages. Intelligent use of large-scale maps will enable you to find these. Examples in this book include routes 5 and 6, which take you to around 1,000 feet without obliging you to get off and push for more than short stretches.

Your Bicycle and its Accessories

A touring bike is of course the thing for a cycle tour, and if you are buying a new machine that is what you will look for. Setting aside costly hand-built jobs, there is still a considerable range of styles and prices to choose from.

My advice is to get your bike from an independent specialist bicycle shop rather than from a chain store or discount warehouse. When you need repairs or servicing, independent shops offer a much more helpful and personal service, and they naturally look askance on people who buy their machines at a cut-price outlet and then come to a proper specialist as soon as something needs attention. Ask cycling friends where the good local shops are, and discuss with the proprietor the best choice of machine for the money you can afford to spend.

If you already have a bicycle, you may wonder if it is OK for a touring holiday. There is not much hope of revamping an old boneshaker. The frame of a touring bike must be of strong, lightweight alloy, and the other elements – pedals, handlebars, brakes, and especially wheels, gears and chainset – must be of correspondingly high quality: otherwise, they may let you down, and their heaviness and inefficiency will in any case add to your labours and detract from your pleasure. It is possible, though, to adapt a sports or 'racing' model (although this is harder with an authentic racing machine): you will need to add mudguards and luggage racks, and modify the gearing.

The gears are a point to note whether you are adapting a

suitable machine or buying a new one. Many off-the-peg models, even touring models, are geared too high, without the good low first and second gears a tourist needs. A laden bicycle is much more comfortably ridden into headwinds and up even slight gradients if you have a really low first gear – I would always go for at least thirty teeth on the largest freewheel cog – which will enable you to keep up a nice steady movement and avoid straining joints and muscles. If you buy a new bike from a specialist shop, the proprietor should be prepared to replace the gears with which it is fitted if these are not low enough.

Five or six gears is a minimum (although if you own a really good quality three-speed machine this might just suffice except on the hillier routes). If buying a new bicycle, I would certainly pay the small extra cost of a double front chainring and changer, which doubles your choice of gears, giving you ten or twelve. A wide selection of ratios, which may seem superfluous on short trips and when you do not have much luggage, is a very worthwhile asset on a tour. By the end of a full day's ride, every one of those ten or twelve speeds will prove to have been just what was needed for some particular stretch of road, some particular combination of wind, gradient and bodily or mental state.

Mountain bikes are popular with some people, and you may wonder how much scope there is for using them in Ireland. Ireland does have a few designated long-distance footpaths, and many dead-end tracks, as well as some forest paths. The snag is that you cannot get hold of maps which show you where these are; and in any case I suspect that they do not amount to an extensive network of through routes. What is more, the metalled lanes are almost car-free in most areas, and will take you into the heart of lonely country on surfaces for which an ordinary touring machine is entirely adequate. It follows that while there may be opportunities for the odd bit of 'rough-stuff' off-the-road riding, a mountain bike is less valuable in Ireland than in Wales or Scotland, where unsurfaced tracks often run for considerable distances and offer attractive alternatives to busy surfaced roads.

Apart from the bicycle itself, additional equipment is needed for a cycle tour, in the form of fittings and bags to carry luggage. You see people riding around with rucksacks on their backs, but this is certainly unsafe and I imagine uncomfortable. The wheel, that great technological breakthrough, removes much of the effort needed to carry heavy weights: why sacrifice its advantages by loading onto your shoulders what you can more easily load onto the bike?

A touring machine will come fitted with at least a rear luggage rack. If you are carrying little gear, rear rack plus panniers, or rear rack plus front rack plus strong bags securely held in place by elastic shock cords, will be enough for everything. If you are camping, or going away for a longish period and wanting to take lots of clothes, you will need luggage racks above both front and rear wheels and at least one set of panniers too. There is a bewildering variety on the market: but whatever style you opt for, you will soon discover that the particular thing you want to lay your hands on at any given moment is buried at the bottom of a bag.

I will tell you what I carried on my last trip to Ireland, and how I stowed it. Like all my Irish trips, this was a camping holiday, and I took a fair amount of gear. It was loaded into front panniers, rear panniers, and miscellaneous bags, as follows:

- *Front panniers*: Plates, cutlery, firelighters, cooking oil, gas stove, cooking vessels (we have a pair of square Army Surplus mess-tins, which show no sign of wear after ten years' use: infinitely superior to 'non-stick' cookware), tin-opener, corkscrew, kettle, salt, pepper, garlic. . . .
- *Atop front rack*: Haversack containing maps, money, travellers' cheques, and some of the day's shopping once we had bought any: in other words, this was the bag full of things that could not be left on the machine when we stopped, and which we took with us when we went to pubs and cafés and around the shops.
- *Atop rear rack*: Sleeping bags, inside a large plastic fertiliser bag (*two* such waterproof bags, one one way round and the other the other, would have been a better idea). Kate took the tent; but a lightweight tent – not a fancy one-hundred-quid job, just a reasonably portable nylon tent – is no great weight even if you have to carry it as well as sleeping bag(s).

  Also on the rear rack, secured by elastic cords running through the handle, was a five-litre water-bottle (a former sunflower oil container). Kate carried a smaller, two-litre bottle: the large one was only filled towards the end of the day, as we began looking for a place to camp. Three litres per person is an adequate allowance for water – so long as you don't wash too much, and assuming that you will be drinking something more tasty – on an overnight camp. During the day, you need only carry a litre or so, enough to cope with sudden thirst.

■ *In the rear panniers*: Ground coffee and filters and filter-cone, thermos flask, bottle(s) of wine, half-litre bottle of whiskey replaced as needful, clothes, washing gear, Richard Ellmann's biography of James Joyce, pump, spare cartridges for gas stove, food supplies, and in the outside pockets of the panniers, spare inner tubes and tool-kit (see *Spares and Repairs* below).

All this, as well as giving you a flavour of what cycle-camping is all about, should show that I do not hold to the view often expressed in cycling manuals that you should weigh (metaphorically if not literally) each item and discard everything not utterly essential. Since I dislike instant coffee, I take with me the equipment for making the real thing. Since a flask of hot tea or coffee is a pleasant and labour-saving enhancement of a mid-morning break, I take a thermos flask.

A cycling holiday is meant to be a pleasure, not a race or an exercise in 'doing without'. It is of course true that 'every pound has to be carried up every hill', but since you and your bike already add up to something from 120 to 180 pounds, a favourite book or jumper makes only a marginal difference. Panniers and carriers give you scope to carry a good deal more than 'bare necessities', and unlike a walker you will not be carrying them on your back.

A final word on the cost of all this. A bike of good quality, plus all necessary additional equipment for a tour, will set you back somewhere between £250 and £320 at 1987 prices. This is a lot of cash to get together at one go – although less than many people spend on a week's holiday, and not a lot more than the return ferry fare for a motor vehicle to Ireland or the Continent. However, a bicycle is an excellent investment, especially if you use it all year round: I would put the annual cost of a bike, *including* depreciation of the capital cost as well as all other expenses, at around £70, for a good machine may well last you ten years and should certainly last you six or seven.

I am not well off, and often wonder how I scraped together the price of my current bike, now five years old; what I do know is that my bicycle – I have no car – is both the best-loved and the most useful of my possessions.

Clothing

It is possible to spend a good deal of money on special cycling kit. Apart from being pricey, this has the further disadvantage that it cannot easily be worn off the bike: I have never bothered with it. However, you will enjoy cycling more if you choose appropriate clothing. For Ireland, apart from a set of clothes (jeans and so on) for the evening, I take the following:

■ *To keep warm/cool*: Both the Irish weather and the body temperature of a cyclist are subject to fluctuations. You need clothes that you can easily peel off/put back on as you move from sunshine to cloud and from uphill to downhill stretches. For your bottom half, a pair of shorts under a pair of tracksuit trousers is ideal: tracksuit trousers can be taken off without trouble once you get warm, and they hold less water and dry out much faster than jeans or cords. For your top half, a long-sleeved sweatshirt, reasonably thick, is cool enough with the sleeves rolled up for all but the hottest Irish days; with the sleeves rolled down, it will keep you comfortably warm most of the time. In chilly weather, and first thing in the morning, you can add a tracksuit top, supplemented either by a thin sweater underneath or a light windproof jacket on top.
■ *On my feet*, I wear training shoes. You need a firm, flat sole, and you will find ordinary plimsoles annoyingly floppy and flexible. Unfortunately, trainers get wet and stay wet: I have seen cyclists wearing ankle-length wellington boots, and I have also heard tell of waterproof cycling overshoes. I don't really mind wet feet, at least not in Ireland's mild temperatures, but I do like to have a pair of dry shoes stowed safely away for the evening. Perhaps waterproof overshoes are the ideal answer; but they would deprive Kate (who *does* mind wet feet) of her favourite evening pastime, a harmless and absorbing activity, which is to hold out her socks to steam perilously dry above the campfire flames.
■ *To keep dry*: At Killybegs in County Donegal, two cyclists who had just got off the long-distance bus from Dublin stood in the pouring rain outside Melly's fish-and-chip shop and discussed with us – as well they might, with the ride to Glencolumbkille before them – the merits of various waterproof gear. This topic is an old favourite among cyclists. There are three alternatives: a waterproof cape, a suit of waterproof jacket plus overtrousers, or an old anorak, nominally 'showerproof', which begins to leak after ten minutes' serious rain. For many years I favoured the third alternative, in the mistaken belief that it was anyhow impossible to keep dry. I now realise how silly this was: wearing a long

cape and a helmet (see *Safety*), I have cycled for hours through heavy rain and insinuating mist, and have stayed quite dry from neck to waist, wearing in the evening the same shirt I had worn all day.

Personally, I prefer a cape because it is well ventilated, so I do not get too sweaty: it will not keep your legs dry, but (as I say) this does not greatly matter if you wear a tracksuit. Other cyclists prefer impermeable jackets and overtrousers. It is a matter of taste, but proper rainproof clothing of one kind or another will add greatly to your pleasure – and resilience – on an Irish cycling holiday.

Safety and Bike-Handling

If you have never done it before, you will need an hour or so to get accustomed to riding a laden bicycle and to acquire the skills and intuitive responses to deal with the extra weight and its unfamiliar distribution. This applies particularly if you are carrying weight above the front wheel. On your first trip, and in the first few hours of every trip, be especially careful not to be caught out by the sheer unexpected heaviness of the machine, by the relatively sluggish feel of the steering, and by the propensity of the handlebars, or indeed the whole bike, to swing suddenly to one side while you stand casually astride the crossbar looking at a map.

On the road and riding, allow extra space for turning and stopping, and plenty of extra reaction time in traffic. Ensure that there is not too much slack in your brake cables, and remember that you will be relying more than usual on the retarding effect of the back brake. It is vital to keep the bike's speed well in check when you are running downhill: it will take a long distance to stop in an emergency once you let your velocity get out of hand. Watch out for uneven or slippery road surfaces: a loaded bike, especially if it is moving fast, will respond catastrophically to a big pothole or to a sharp corner on loose gravel. If you are in a group, take care to keep well apart from each other, and remember those classic Tour de France pile-ups when one rider touches another's wheel and fifty more come down in their wake.

The number one safety rule is more easily observed in Ireland than in any other country that I know. It is: avoid busy roads. Ten minutes in thick fast-moving traffic is tolerable, if inadvisable, but a longer period makes heavy and unwelcome demands on your concentration and bike-handling. Remember that if you fall off on a lane, you will probably escape with minor cuts and bruises, but that if you fall off on a main road there may be a truck behind you. I emphasise this because I have seen cycling guidebooks that seriously recommend routes involving 'B' and even 'A' roads in Britain – roads that I would regard, certainly in the built-up parts of the country, as both dangerous and horrible. In Ireland, however, you would have to be wilfully perverse to find such roads or stay on them: once away from the major cities, traffic will not bother you (a point which I elaborate in chapter 3).

I wear a helmet, a sturdy one, whenever I ride my bicycle. This began after I sailed inattentively into the back of a parked Telecom van in twilit Brighton: catching my head on a projecting ladder, I was lucky to escape with just three stitches. Helmets can be a little irritating in warm weather (I take mine off on long climbs, since at three or four mph it is hardly necessary) although to compensate for this, they offer excellent protection against the rain, deflecting onto your back and shoulders the drips and cascades that otherwise make their way via your hair and neck to your chest. If you fall off at speed or ride into something, they might just save your life.

One last safety point: mountain lanes in Ireland can be quite deserted, so that you might break down and spend many hours before a vehicle came past. If cycling alone, I would not choose to set off into empty country in really wet weather, especially towards evening. In any case, you should always be sure, before embarking on a long stretch of empty lanes, that you have a supply of energy-giving, easily eaten food with you.

All this has begun to sound alarming. Provided you use common sense and keep a watch on the condition of your bicycle there is nothing to be alarmed about, however. Experience will show you that cycle-touring is as safe as it is pleasant, and with experience confidence will come.

Spares and Repairs

Bike repair shops are few and far between in most of Ireland, and public transport infrequent or non-existent on smaller roads. It is important, then, that you should be able to repair your bicycle in the event of breakdown – although in an emergency you could no doubt get a local farmer to run you and your bike a few miles on a trailer.

'In the event of breakdown': but breakdowns are by no means inevitable, and should not occur at all if you leave with the bicycle in good condition. Prevention is better than cure. I love cycle-touring and I admire and respect my bicycle, but I dislike messing about with greasy chains and recalcitrant spoke nipples – especially on holiday. Over the years I have put together a check-list of things to watch for and if necessary to fix or get fixed before setting out on a tour. Don't leave repairs and servicing until the last minute : if you need the attention of a professional repairer, you will find that the summer months are busy, and you may have to wait awhile before your bike can be fitted in.

Things to watch for, then, include:

■ *Chainset and drive-train*: Once freewheel blocks and chains begin to wear down perceptibly, they degenerate fast, and the bicycle can become unrideable, with the chain slipping on the block, within days. Keep a close eye on the teeth of your freewheel block and be sure that there is no tendency for the chain to 'jump' (if it does, it will be when in high gear and/or when you are exerting sudden or heavy pressure on the pedals). If the block and chain are clearly wearing out, replace them before you go.

If your bicycle is more than three years old, it is worth taking it along to a trusted repair shop and asking whether the chainset (front chain-rings plus bottom bracket assembly) could do with replacing: both the chainring teeth and the bottom bracket bearings are subject to intense stresses and will not last indefinitely.

■ *Pedals*: Listen out for clicks, and feel for 'sticky patches'. If pedals do not spin freely and quietly on their spindles, replace them, for they too can go quickly from bad to worse if you start with them in poor condition.

■ *Wheels*: One of the best investments a cycle-tourist can make is to have a rear wheel hand-built by a trusted repairer. Especially if you are large or heavy, and if you carry a lot of gear, a hand-built wheel is a boon, being less likely than an off-the-peg one to suffer from spoke breakages and distortions.

Whether your wheels are hand-built or not, look them over before leaving and see that they are well trued up, with the spokes all under even tension. (This applies especially to the rear wheel: front wheels carry less weight and do less work, and rarely give problems.)

■ *Brakes, gears, cables*: Check cables to brakes and gears, and replace them if they show any sign of fraying. Fit new brake blocks. If the gear mechanism is more than three or four years old, consider whether it should be replaced: take an expert's advice, or if you are experienced you can judge this for yourself by sensing the amount of play in the mechanism and thus the degree to which the spring is losing its resilience.

■ *Tyres*: In the summer of 1987 I cycled well over 1,000 miles in Ireland without a single puncture, and there is nothing exceptional or mysterious about this. Punctures do sometimes happen, but their frequency will be much reduced if you fit new outer tubes ('covers') just before setting out on a tour (the worn ones can of course be kept and used again in due course). Not only are new covers thicker, their fabric is more resistant and resilient.

If you check all these parts of your bicycle, and replace them if necessary (which will not be the case most years), you should have a trouble-free holiday. However, you do need to be able to fix the commonest kinds of breakdown. Apart from replacing a punctured tube, you should know how to replace gear and brake cables; remove links in the chain (if the chain breaks, you need to take out the broken link plus its neighbour in order to fit it together again); carry out routine adjustments to brakes and gears (you *must* keep your gears adjusted so that it is impossible for the mechanism to tangle with the spokes as you change down into first); and remove and replace broken spokes. This last operation is tricky when, as usually happens, the broken spoke is in the rear wheel on the same side as the freewheel block: you have to remove the block before the job can be done (see route 6 for an account of how I fared).

Major breakdowns, involving the bottom bracket, the headset (steering assembly), or serious damage to the wheels, are beyond the scope of roadside repairs: should you be so unlucky as to meet with them, you will have to get yourself and your bicycle transported, somehow, to the nearest bike shop, rail station or bus depot. However, there is no reason to anticipate bad luck of that kind. In twelve years of cycle-touring, I have never had to abandon a holiday, and such mechanical mishaps as I have suffered from have been the result of my own inattention to the excellent advice I have given above.

What spares and tools will you need to take? Obviously,

whatever is required for the repairs and adjustments I have listed. This means:

- screwdrivers, allen keys and spanners/adjustable spanner (get a good quality one) to fit all the screws and bolts on your bike;
- freewheel block remover, spoke key (again, avoid cheap, useless models), spokes of the right size (a total of five or six spokes will be enough);
- chain rivet extractor;
- tyre levers, puncture repair kit, three or four spare inner tubes (it is easier to replace the tube than to repair a puncture at the side of the road: the punctured tube can be fixed that evening, or when you get home);
- spare cables cut to length for front and rear brakes and gears: make sure that you have the right kind of nipple (barrel or pear-shaped) on these, and get the shopkeeper to cut off the 'wrong end' with his/her wirecutters, since you will not be carrying wirecutters good enough to snip through a cable and leave a clean, frayless end;
- small bottle of oil, spare brakeblocks, small pair of pliers, length of galvanised wire for emergency repairs.

Some cyclists carry a spare outer cover just in case a giant nail or savage flint rips a hole right through their tyres. I do not bother with this when I am on my own, but if two or more of you have the same size tyres, you might consider taking a spare cover between you: rolled into three overlapping circles, it will not take up much space.

Going to Ireland: Passports, Currency

British citizens travelling between Britain and the Republic of Ireland do not need passports, but if you have a passport you would be well advised to take it with you since it is the most acceptable proof of identity: you could be asked to give such proof, especially on your return to Britain. If you are a citizen of any other country, or if you travel to Ireland from anywhere other than Britain, you will need a passport.

Irish currency, like British, is divided into pounds (*punts*) and pence: the punt (IR£) is currently (1987) worth about 8% less than the £ sterling. Irish banks close at lunchtime, but stay open later in the afternoon than British ones. Some restaurants, hotels and Bed and Breakfasts will accept, and give change for, travellers' cheques, as will some post offices in remote but touristic areas: don't rely on this, however. In most parts of Ireland, you are bound to pass a couple of banks in a day's ride, for any town large enough to have a range of shops will usually also have a bank. But where I warn you, in the route texts, that shopping facilities are limited, you should assume that there is no bank, and plan ahead accordingly.

British currency is not legal tender in the Republic. However, British banknotes will often be accepted, especially if you are happy to ignore the exchange rate and offer them on a 'pound-for-punt' basis.

Transport to and around Ireland

I have always travelled by train and ship when visiting Ireland with my bike, but there are alternatives.

Airlines will usually accept a bicycle as part of your luggage allowance, but you will probably have to take off the pedals and turn the handlebars through 90 degrees. Air travel will save a lot of time if you are coming from the Continent or further afield, and it does give you the option of westerly landings at Cork, Shannon or (God preserve us!) Knock, County Mayo.

Within Ireland, a network of buses, local services and long-distance express routes, compensates for the rather vestigial train service. As well as being cheaper than trains, buses will take you into areas such as Clare, west Cork and Donegal where the railway does not run. Bord Failte (see *Maps and Guides*, chapter 3) will advise you on the best way to book ahead: you should certainly do this to ensure that space is reserved for your machine. The couple we met at Killybegs explained that when they turned up at Dublin bus station, nobody seemed to have heard about their advance booking or their bikes, but since they insisted that they *had* booked ahead, the driver very happily made room for their machines – not in the boot, which was already full, but inside the coach itself. . . .

By train and ship, you can leave Britain via Swansea, Fishguard, Holyhead/Liverpool or Stranraer, arriving in Cork, Rosslare, Dublin/Dun Laoghaire and Larne (Northern Ireland, but connecting via Belfast with Dublin trains). Travel agents will have up-to-date fares and timetables. Before making your choice of route, there are a couple of points which cyclists should bear in mind. The South Wales ports are served by Inter-City 125 trains, which means that you must reserve space for your bicycle and pay a small supplement (currently £3 each way): neither the reservation nor the supplement applies to the Holyhead and Liverpool services. Whichever route you travel, there is also a charge on the boat for your bike (currently £4 each way).

Cork, Rosslare and Dun Laoghaire are all delightful landfalls, and from any of them you can be in open country and enjoying your holiday within half an hour of disembarking. It is worth noting, though, that Dublin is the most suitable point to pick up train services, not just to the west and north-west, but even to more southern towns such as Kilkenny or Thurles. If you are planning to travel some way west by train, it will save money to buy a through ticket from Britain. You will have to pay for your bicycle on Irish trains (one quarter of the adult fare is charged), but there is no need to reserve space.

If you are travelling via Dun Laoghaire, you must remember that there is no accommodation for bicycles on the surburban trains that run into Dublin city: allow an hour to reach the mainline stations by bike.

Hotels, Bed and Breakfasts, Camping

Leopold Bloom's father Rudolph, in *Ulysses*, takes poison in a hotel in Ennis. Hotels in one or two Irish towns have plunged me into a severe, though less than suicidal, gloom: dusty corridors and uncleaned bathrooms proved an all too telling presage of memorably greasy breakfasts. It is as well to avoid these decaying relics, stranded by a long-ebbed tide of inland commerce, whose shortcomings are often well known to the local population: in one town in Cork, we crossed the street from our hotel, shivering from our 'hot' shower, and went into a bar for a reviving drink. And how did we feel, the young barman asked us, when we looked about ourselves in the W— Arms? We were politely evasive, but the barman was less reticent: 'I'd have been overwhelmed,' he assured us, 'with dismay'.

So you may not get very good value if you stay in a run-down hotel in an out-of-the-way town. But in most of Ireland, and in all the touristic areas, there is a wide choice of Bed and Breakfast accommodation, and this I have always found to be friendly, clean and inexpensive. Bord Failte publishes a list of approved B and Bs, and these make a standard charge: for IR£10, in 1987, we had bed, breakfast, and a shower en suite. 'Unapproved' B and Bs are slightly cheaper and correspondingly less luxurious, although they can also be rather friendlier and less formal. Book ahead if you are relying on a B and B in a remote area (the Bord Failte brochure has telephone numbers, and any tourist office in Ireland will help you book a room); in towns, there is less need to bother – even in August I have never failed to find a suitable place.

I have not stayed in Irish Youth Hostels, which are often set in remote places. They are said to be more spartan, but more relaxed, than their British counterparts. As well as 'official' hostels affiliated to the IYHA, for which you will need a membership card of your national Association, there are in Ireland several 'independent' hostels: I have no experience of these. They offer simple accommodation and facilities for you to prepare your own food.

As I have said, I invariably take a tent to Ireland. Official campsites are not numerous, but no country that I have visited offers such splendid scope for 'wild camping'. In the more intensively cultivated areas, you will need to ask a farmer's permission to camp in a field: I have never met with anything but the friendliest welcome. Further west and in upland areas, there are many most beautiful spots – beside a lough, on a stretch of moorland or open rough grazing, at the edge of a peatbog, on the wide grassy verge of a quiet lane – where you can pitch a tent confident that if any local inhabitant does pass by, they will be delighted to see you, and will probably stop for a talk. Irish attitudes to land ownership and 'trespassing' are infinitely more relaxed, democratic and accommodating than what you will encounter in Britain. This imposes on you an obligation not to abuse the opportunities that this lovely land offers you: make very certain to leave no rubbish behind you.

The Irish climate is likely to test the waterproof qualities of your tent, but it also has compensating advantages. It is a rare summer that is dry enough to entail any risk of fire, so you need not feel anxious about lighting a campfire, although obviously you should not do so in the depths of a wood. You will often find water close at hand when you pitch your tent. In remote areas, I happily drink from streams and loughs (you may well see a small pumping station taking drinking water from a mountain lake). Don't drink from rivers in more agricultural parts: every time I visit Ireland there is some newspaper report about pollution from pig slurry or sileage effluent.

Food and Drink

Cycling induces a hearty appetite, and makes you properly appreciative of simple food, so long as it is good. The range of choice in Irish shops, especially in smaller towns, is often limited, but quality is excellent: superb butter, good cheese, and bread – both soda bread and white bread – that often puts the average British (and indeed French) loaf to shame. If you are not a vegetarian, you will appreciate the quality, and low price, of Irish meat, for this is a stock-raising and a carnivorous country, although modern notions of 'healthy eating' are catching on: to the consternation, I have no doubt, of Irish farmers and economic planners. Sea and freshwater fish is caught in quantity in Ireland, but it can be surprisingly difficult to find anywhere that sells it: at Ballinrobe, near Lough Mask, as famed a trout water as any in the country, the only supplier of fish was a butcher who sold it just three days a week.

Vegetables are often restricted to basics: potatoes and carrots (both generally of good quality), onions, lettuce, tomatoes. In larger towns, the spread of supermarkets, which has gathered pace markedly since I first visited Ireland, is changing this: the supermarkets remain small by British standards, but offer a better choice of vegetables than the one-room general stores they are displacing.

From the cyclist's point of view, the great thing about shops in Ireland is their wide distribution. In less inhabited areas, even tiny villages often have a general store. Any town whose name appears in capitals on the Ordnance Survey map is likely to have a baker, a butcher, and a small supermarket or two. You will generally pass through at least one such town in a day's ride: if there are problems with shopping in any of the routes described, your attention is drawn to them in the route text.

Irish shops tend to open later, and close later, than their British counterparts. You will usually find some shops open on a Sunday between Mass and lunchtime, although larger supermarkets, and most specialist shops, will stay closed. Ask locally about half-day closing in country areas, or else make a point of shopping in the morning – although it is my impression that half-day closing is rare nowadays, and in sizeable towns you will certainly find shops open every afternoon of the week.

When it comes to eating out, Ireland is much like Britain. In larger and more touristic places, you will find expensive gourmet restaurants, some of which have a reputation (myself, I am not into that kind of eating). Every cyclist will be concerned, though, to know what kind of basic roadside sustenance is on offer, and here the choice lies between pubs and cafés. Cafés and tea-shops are found only in larger towns: they usually offer sandwiches and salads as well as the massive fried meals which I confess to enjoying after a couple of hours' hard ride. Pubs are less widely scattered in the countryside than they are in Britain: if you do find one, it will usually offer sandwiches and soup. In remote areas don't rely on finding a suitable pub: take some food with you, even if it is wet and you hope that you will not have to picnic.

Irish people will tell you that theirs is a dear country, apologising to the English visitor and saying that high prices keep tourists away. I cannot see that this is a justifiable generalisation: once you have made allowance for the exchange rate, worth almost 10 pence in the pound, Irish shop prices are only marginally higher than British. The main exceptions are alcohol and tobacco (and petrol), all taxed quite a bit more heavily than they are in Britain.

Wine is particularly expensive: a reasonable bottle cost a minimum of around £3 in 1987. If you drink wine regularly, you may think it worth bringing some in your panniers, either from some cheaper country or from the ship or airport duty-free shop. Despite its relatively high price, wine seems to be increasingly drunk in the Republic, and in the years since I first went there it has become much easier to find. You may be unlucky, however, and find that the choice is 'tonic wine' or nothing: in which case you can always buy some Guinness.

3

ROADS AND LANES,
MAPS AND GUIDES

It is difficult to imagine a road network more perfectly adapted to the cyclist's needs and preferences than the one you will find in Ireland. Anyone who has cycled there will recall the endless miles of empty lanes and the lack of traffic even on the classified highways.

Ireland's dispersed rural population and fundamentally agricultural economy mean that outside the wildest upland areas a web of surfaced lanes links villages, hamlets and scattered farmsteads. The lanes are sometimes bumpy and occasionally there are loose gravelly stretches, but an ordinary touring bike is well able to cope with them. They are mostly quite narrow, but this scarcely matters since you will often ride for many miles without encountering a single car or tractor.

Although the classified roads are busier, very few of them are anywhere near as crowded as a typical 'B' road in most of Britain. Lanes bring you into a more intimate relationship with the lie of the land, and their narrower gauge and lack of wide verges make them less intrusive on the countryside: in Ireland as elsewhere, they are the cyclist's preferred choice, and nearly every route in this book makes extensive use of them. However, there is no need (as there is in more populous and industrial countries) positively to avoid classified roads, and these do have advantages if you want to make rapid and straightforward progress: see, for instance, my comments on route 11.

The only routes that are really inhospitable to the cyclist are the main National highways linking Dublin to the provincial cities of Wexford, Waterford, Cork, Limerick, Galway and Sligo. You will also be well advised to avoid main roads immediately around these provincial cities, and to keep as far as possible to lanes in the touristic highspots during the busiest season. On the very few occasions that routes in this book make any use of relatively crowded roads, this is mentioned in the text.

Road Classification

For some years now, the Irish system of road classification has been in the process of revision. This process does not seem to be nearing completion. Eventually – *mañana*, a sceptic might say – the aim is to replace the present unwieldy classification with a comprehensive nationwide division into numbered National and Regional roads.

Meanwhile, the Ordnance Survey (OS) maps (see below) have not yet begun to employ the new classification except in the case of the major National roads. Away from these roads, it is rare to see any on-the-ground indication of the route numbers, old or new. I have accordingly avoided using classificatory numbers in my routes and sketch maps, except in the case of the major through ways. I have, however, distinguished between 'classified roads' in general and 'lanes'. Most lanes, or 'third class roads', are shown in yellow on the OS maps. The smallest lanes, or 'other roads', are uncoloured.

This broad distinction between 'lanes' and 'classified roads' may be subject to some slight change whenever the new system becomes visibly operative, since a few of the wider lanes are being recategorised as Regional roads (broadly analogous to the French 'D' roads). However, given the small number of lanes likely to be so affected, and the slow pace at which the Irish Ordnance Survey is able to update its classification, the distinction I use will remain valid for many years to come.

Roadsigns

Once you venture off the classified roads, which as a rule are easy to follow, with clear route indications at junctions and inter-sections, you will find yourself in Ireland at the mercy of a 'system' of signposts as variable and potentially baffling as you may expect in the rural areas of any country. Connoisseurs of little-used byways will know what to anticipate. A turning off a main road may be boldly signposted 'Castlerea', and may then fork, a mile further on, into two equally plausible-looking continuations with no guidance as to which you should take. One signpost may choose to indicate some intermediate destination, and the next may revert to a more distant but larger settlement. You may pass, as we did, a milepost reading 'Castlerea 4', climb a long and tiring hill, swoop down a welcome descent, do another good mile on the flat, and pass another signpost reading 'Castlerea 4' (and neither of these signposts was in kilometres). If this does happen, it will be towards the end of a stiff ride, when you are longing for a rest and a bite to eat, or hurrying to catch a train.

None of this seriously detracts from the pleasure of finding your own way through mazelike lanes – on a good day, when you are unhurried, mishaps can be a pleasure in themselves – but it does emphasise the need for careful map reading. The rule here is to keep track of every turning off your route, and when in doubt about which way to go, trust the map. The map may very occasionally be inaccurate – but it is less error-prone than you are, and you would do well to adopt the sentiment quoted in J H Andrews' *A Paper Landscape*, a fascinating history of nineteenth-century Ordnance Survey map-making in Ireland: 'Believe me, I think two or three times before venturing to pick a hole in any of the ordnance work which may almost be deemed infallible, so few are the errors.'

Irish signposts have certain peculiarities of their own. The most striking, and potentially baffling, is the concurrent use – sometimes on a single signpost – of kilometres and statute miles. Kilometric distances are preferred on the green-and-yellow route-signs of the National roads (this is a conscious policy of 'European-isation', a counterweight to the mark England has left on Ireland). Elsewhere, miles are more usually – but by no means always – given, and Irish people are no more likely than English people spontaneously to give a distance in kilometres. The moral for the cyclist is not to grow downcast when the late breakfast or early lunch you have been looking forward to suddenly retreats into the distance: if you see a '12' where you had sworn there would be a '7', the signpost which has dismayed you is probably a metric one.

In Gaeltacht areas (where the population is predominantly, or at least 'officially', Irish-speaking), place-names are given solely in their Irish form. Often this poses only slight problems: 'Conga' is pretty obviously 'Cong', and if you are expecting to reach Ballingeary soon, you may well guess that you have arrived when you see the signboard that says Beal Atha an Ghaorthaidh. But where the two names are unrelated, as in the case of Clonbur/An Fhairche, no amount of etymological cunning is likely to reveal that they belong to the same place. Nor does the OS map help, since even in Gaeltacht areas it gives only the English place-name of smaller settlements (larger towns are always given both English and Irish names). Again, however, all this is fun, giving you the sense of being in a foreign country (although this partly artificial, state-sponsored 'Irishness' is not what makes Ireland really, radically foreign). Maps and common sense will keep you on the right road in the Gaeltacht as elsewhere. And if you do get lost for a few miles, will it matter?

Maps

I do not have strong opinions on most of the issues which bike-freaks like to disagree about: ten versus twelve gears, centre- versus side-pull brakes. I do, however, have strong views about maps, and I regard maps of a sufficiently large scale as indispensable equipment for a really enjoyable cycle-tour.

The readily available ½-inch (1:126,720) Irish Ordnance Survey maps are in many respects ideal for the cyclist (the larger, one-inch map is virtually unobtainable). Half a mile to the inch allows every lane, and many dead-end tracks, to be shown, and gives space for the inclusion of minor place-names, churches, and other aids to navigation. On the other hand, the scale is small enough for a good stretch of country, fifty by thirty-five miles, to appear on each sheet. With contours at 100-foot intervals, the lie of the land can be quite accurately determined: it is true that where there are small switchback hills, the road may run up and down over them without crossing contour lines, but this is not a serious problem. The colour-layering used to show relief makes the shape of the land spring to the eye, and also produces a very attractive map aesthetically. Some of the OS sheets, where blue lakes and blue sea run in among pasture and mountain, are used as wall decorations by exiles and others homesick for the Irish countryside. Map 10, Connemara, is a favourite. The map of west Cork, sheet 24, is also striking, prompting a friend of mine to comment: 'It looks lovely – I've never seen Ireland so close up.'

Cartographically, these maps are no doubt inferior to the British 1:50,000 series: Andrews, in *A Paper Landscape*, says that they are 'recognisably derived from the map of 1912–18', and while they do of course undergo periodical revision, this does not happen all that frequently. Each map has a note to tell you when it was last revised, and you should note this before trusting its depiction of railways, many of which have been axed since the early 1970s. There have been fewer changes of significance in the road network, although in one case (route 10) I have drawn your attention to highway 'improvements' not yet shown on the map.

I always use the OS ½-inch series, and as explained below I refer to these maps in my route texts. However, there are alternatives which, while they do not in my view give the detail you really need, are just about adequate. Both the Irish Ordnance Survey and Bartholomew Ltd produce a set of maps at 1:250,000 (the Bartholomew set is at a quarter of a mile to the inch, or 1:253,440 to be precise). Showing most lanes, and all classified roads, these cover Ireland in four or five sheets, as compared to the 25 sheets of the ½-inch series. This obviously makes them cheaper, and means that fewer maps are needed to cover a large area.

The Irish Ordnance Survey also issues a map depicting the entire country, North and South, on a single sheet at a scale of nine miles to the inch. It shows the classified roads, and in remoter areas gives a selection of lanes too, although few lanes can be shown in more populous parts. The nine-miles-to-the-inch map is not recommended as the sole basis for navigating, but it does have two uses. It is helpful when you are planning your overall itinerary, allowing you to see the country as a whole without switching constantly from map to map. It is useful, too, in finding direct routes across from one area to another – from Dublin, say, across the midlands to the Shannon. Provided you stick to minor classified roads, you can plot a course on it that will keep you away from heavy traffic.

My own advice is to use the nine-miles-to-the-inch map for long cross-country stretches, and then switch to the ½-inch map for touring in the region where you will spend most of your holiday. If you are visiting, say, Mayo and Connemara, just three of the larger scale maps (numbers 6, 10 and 11) will give you the detail you need. This way you can build up, as I have done, a collection of ½-inch maps gradually over the years – a collection which will be not just useful but pleasantly evocative, bringing to mind the Irish countryside when on a winter evening you sit over your maps and dream of the cycle-tour you may make next summer.

Guidebooks

So far as I know, there exists no guidebook designed specifically for cycle-touring in Ireland. There is a selection of routes in the *Cyclists' Touring Club Route Guide to Britain and Ireland* (edited by Christa Gausden and Nicholas Crane), and Bord Failte issues a series of information sheets that suggest itineraries as well as listing shops where you can hire a bicycle. Neither of these offers a lot of detail or a full sense of the landscape, but both will give you some ideas. You may also like to know that Bike Events of Bath organise cycling holidays in Ireland: a travel agent should be able to put you in the picture about these.

There are, of course, many guidebooks compiled with the general tourist – that is, the motorist – in mind. Some of these are regularly updated (the AA, for instance, have just reissued their volume). I have found the *Blue Guide* particularly, if prosaically, thorough and informative: it is not currently in print, but you may find a copy in your local library. If you want a comprehensive guide or gazetteer to the entire country, and especially if you want to look up details of archaeological and historic sites, it is obviously a good idea to spend a few hours with one of the standard guides before you set off.

Bord Failte issues annual brochures covering accommodation, special events (musical and other festivals), eating out in Ireland, camping and caravanning parks, and so on. There is a charge for these, but their annual 'Inclusive Holidays' guide is free. Bord Failte's British office is at 150 New Bond Street, London W1; the Dublin office is in Baggot Street Bridge. You will find their staff friendly and helpful. They can give you addresses of railway and bus offices and the like.

You may also want to note two other addresses. The Irish Youth Hostels Association (An Oige) is at 39 Mountjoy Square, Dublin 1. If you cannot obtain Irish maps locally, write to Stanford's Ltd of 12–14 Long Acre, London WC2.

Many travellers have written more personal or literary accounts of their journeying in Ireland since Thackeray exhorted his fellow-Britons to visit it, praising the country near Westport in terms which suggest that the 'tourist industry' was already establishing itself in the 1840s – and that Ireland was neglected then as it is now:

It forms an event in one's life to have seen that place, so beautiful is it, and so unlike all other beauties that I know of. Were such beauties lying upon English shores it would be a world's wonder: perhaps, if it were on the Mediterranean, or the Baltic, English travellers would flock to it by hundreds; why not come and see it in Ireland?

Despite the poverty which then oppressed the Irish people, and which soon after his visit culminated in the catastrophic famine, Thackeray was captivated by the country, and many subsequent writers have shared his enthusiasm. I have looked at no more than a small sample of this literature. Sean Jennett's books on *Connacht* and *Munster* are full of historical information. Benedict Kiely's *All the Way to Bantry Bay* has much literary and antiquarian anecdote. Again, it is worth visiting your local bookshop or library to see what is on offer.

As well as guidebooks, there are scholarly volumes dealing with Ireland's geology, geography and history. I hesitate to recommend historical works, since the subject is controversial and I have read only introductory studies. Of geographical and geological accounts, I would particularly mention Frank Mitchell's *The Irish Landscape*, although like most of the books I have referred to it will take on a deeper meaning only when you have made first-hand acquaintance of the country that it describes.

Using this Book

The rest of this book consists of twenty-two detailed descriptions of routes through some of Ireland's most exciting cycling country. Cyclists tend to be independent spirits, and I do not expect to curb your native inventiveness: indeed, no attempt is made to provide a country-wide network of linked routes, for I assume that you will want, much of the time, to be left to your own maps and your own devices. I hope that the routes, and my descriptions of them, will inspire you to make discoveries of your own.

The routes are all in some way memorable, and most of them are too delightful to be missed. I have given sufficient detail to allow each one to be followed (with the aid, of course, of a map). Each route description is preceded by the number of the relevant OS ½-inch sheet(s); the sheet title(s), which will allow you to find the route on other published maps; a note of the route's location; and a full summary of the itinerary. In more complicated cases, a sketch-map is provided too, as an additional aid to navigation and to the armchair traveller. These sketch-maps can give only an outline of the route, for the scale practicable in such a book as this does not permit every turning off to be shown (although all relevant classified road junctions are marked). When looking at the sketch-maps, check their scale, for not all are drawn to the same scale.

And so – *bon voyage*!: or should I not rather say, as a young Donegal farm-woman said when Kate and I thanked her for the eggs she had given us, 'a thousand welcomes and a thousand welcomes' to a landscape which you will never forget if once you visit it.

4
MOUNTAINS:
the south

Routes 1–6

Route 1:
Bunclody to Inistioge – The Blackstairs Mountains

OS 19 (Carlow–Wexford). Distance: approx. 27 miles

Location: Bunclody is about 50m SSW of Dublin, and is situated on the river Slaney at the border between County Carlow and County Wexford. Inistioge is a village in the valley of the river Nore, about 15m SE of Kilkenny town.

Itinerary: From Bunclody, SSW – on the classified road or on lanes just to its W – via Doran's Crossroads to Kiltealy (8m). Follow the classified road through Scullogue Gap to Graiguenamanagh (20m). Leave Graigue-namanagh on the New Ross road, but fork right less than 1m out of town and follow lanes over to Inistioge (27m).

Riding south-west out of Dublin or Dun Laoghaire, you will come, as you leave the Wicklow massif behind you, to the narrow Blackstairs range – no rival in height or extent to the mountains you have been crossing, but with its own particular charm, its single chain of peaks rising gracefully above the surrounding valleys.

In clear conditions there is a magnificent panoramic view from the top of Mount Leinster, at 2,610 feet the tallest of the group: you can climb there from the Nine Stones six miles west of Bunclody. The sea and the high tops of Wicklow glisten to the east and north, while away to the west the dark shapes of range after mountain range – Slieve Bloom, Slievenamon, the Galtees – rise from the green plain. A prospect full of enticing charm if you are setting out on your travels, and full of melancholy if you are about to leave Ireland. . . . However, the ride (or push) up to the Nine Stones is a stiff job. If you are staying nearby, at Bunclody perhaps or Graiguenamanagh (where there is a Youth Hostel), the expedition to the summit makes a memorable trip, but you should allow a full day for it.

The route I have chosen crosses the Blackstairs range four miles south of Mount Leinster. It is much less demanding than the Nine

Stones pass, rising to less than 700 feet: coming from the east – down out of Wicklow, perhaps, by Shillelagh, Clonegall and Bunclody – a moderately fit cyclist will be able to ride the whole way over this modest col without dismounting.

Bunclody, with its wide streets and gravelled public garden and fountain, has a slightly continental flavour. The afternoon we were there, it reminded me of somewhere in the Auvergne, grey and slaty, lying in the shadow of darkly impressive hills. A dramatic hailstorm brought out glistening, ominous tones in the trees, the buildings, the broad river Slaney and the looming mountain backdrop: the ride ahead of us, which we could see from the map presented no real challenge, seemed for a moment thrilling and difficult.

South from Bunclody towards Kiltealy (like many Irish villages, this is a place-name on a map rather than a single nucleus of dwellings), you can follow the quiet classified road or take lanes just to the west of it part of the way. At Doran's Crossroads, where the Enniscorthy turning branches off to the left, I had that improbable accident, a lucky puncture. I took my bike off the road at the first convenient point, the entrance (so it turned out) of a grassy glade at the top of a little wood above a charming, clear, clay-and-pebble-bedded stream, whose admittedly unprepossessing name is the Urrin River. It was after five o'clock, we were tired, it was not at all clear that we would find as good a spot higher into the hills, so we decided to camp here. By the time I had put a new tube in my tyre – I am a slow worker – Kate had pitched the tent and lit the fire, and water for tea was almost boiling. Sitting here after supper, we looked westwards to the long line of the Blackstairs ridge and that most familiar Irish evening sight, streams of cloud trailing away from the sunset over a pale, clearing sky.

Next morning we set off over the Blackstairs. As the road climbs through the Scullogue Gap, there is a brief sense of mountain life, with stone-walled sheep pastures rising away on either side, but before long you are dropping down again into the valley of the Barrow. Only later, when you look back from further west, do the Blackstairs assume sentinel-like prominence as the southernmost outcrop of the Leinster granite: from near at hand, less favoured by long perspectives, they are just another pretty ridge.

The Barrow at Graiguenamanagh ('Granary of the Monks') is an impressive stretch of water, with a deeper navigation channel cut against the east bank. This allows passage to pleasure craft (it was originally constructed for barges), and you may see a cruiser or two moored here as you cross the stone bridge into the tightly built, rather cramped little town. I do not know whether Graiguenamanagh is much visited by sleek, white launches of the kind found all down the Shannon from Carrick to Lough Derg: as Kate and I sat drinking coffee on a riverside bench, watching the sleepy comings and goings of Sunday morning, we remarked that most of the boats we could see looked too dilapidated to travel far. The navigation channel, with occasional locks where the main water-course tumbles over rapids, links Waterford, on the Barrow estuary, by way of Athy to the Grand Canal running from Dublin to the Shannon. In Ireland as in Britain, leisure and tourism are bringing a shadow of liveliness to inland waterways, long since moribund so far as freight transport goes.

Leaving Graiguenamanagh on the main road for New Ross and Waterford, you turn off right a little out of town and climb sharply out of the valley across the northern slopes of Brandon Hill (1,703 feet), soon dropping down into another river valley, that of the Nore, which flows into the Barrow above New Ross. Here too, at Inistioge, you cross a fine stone eighteenth-century bridge, with the village clustered attractively round a green on the west bank. This compact, integrated layout, unusual in Ireland, adds to the charm of this delightfully situated place.

Route 2:
Slievenamon to Araglin, by Clonmel

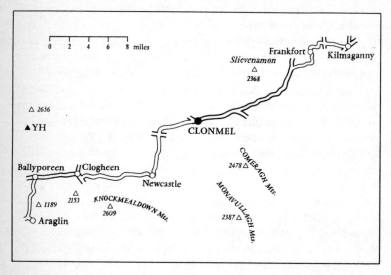

OS 18 (Tipperary) and 22 (East Cork, Waterford). Distance: approx. 52 miles

Location: Kilmaganny is in County Kilkenny, about 18m NW of Waterford. Clonmel lies in the valley of the river Suir, north of the Comeragh, Monavullagh and Knockmealdown mountains. The Araglin valley runs into the Kilworth Mountains towards the Knockmealdowns, south of a ridge facing the Galtees.

Itinerary: From Kilmaganny, follow lanes W along the foot of the Slievenamon ridge, crossing the classified Callan–Carrick-on-Suir road before turning left (5m) to climb on lanes over the ridge near Frankfort. Drop down by way of lanes to join the Callan–Clonmel road, which in turn feeds into the N24 (Carrick-on-Suir–Clonmel). Beyond Clonmel (23m), follow the north bank of the Suir along lanes to Newcastle (32m). Cross the Suir and keep on lanes immediately S of this river, and of its tributary the Tar, to Clogheen (42m). Then take the classified road towards Mitchelstown, but turn off left at Ballyporeen (47m) to climb by lanes over the Kilworth ridge and down to Araglin (52m).

Slievenamon, near where this route starts, and Ballyporeen, near where it finishes, are associated with widely contrasting myths. It was up the steep slopes of Slievenamon that Grainne outraced her rivals to win the hand of the legendary Finn MacCoul: it is easy to see how legends clung and grew around this isolated cone rising to almost 2,400 feet out of the Tipperary Vale. Ballyporeen, by contrast, was the birthplace of Ronald Reagan's grandfather, and thanks to the President's visit in 1984 the village boasts a Ronald Reagan Museum, while car windscreens for miles around sport green sunstrips with the slogan: 'Have you seen Ballyporeen?'

This, I suppose, is a piece of American mythology: the search for roots, at once real and imaginary. But an outsider is struck by how much Ireland's own identity seems confirmed by presidential and senatorial visits and ancestries. Given the numbers who have emigrated to the New World in the famine years and since, given the support Irish-Americans have lent to the struggle for independence, and given also the importance of tourist dollars today, links between the two countries are obviously strong. Still, it is disconcerting to find displayed proudly and prominently outside some roadside bar a sign declaring (in effect) 'Edward Kennedy stopped here for a drink'. Much of Ireland's character is bound up with its military non-alignment, which makes it in some crucial respects *less* American not only than Britain but even than Italy. For all its bitter history, most of southern Ireland offers to the traveller a landscape extraordinarily pacific, blessedly free of the V-bomber and F-111 airfields, early warning aerials, bunkers, military training grounds and nuclear power stations which those of us across the water have somehow to accept as part of our countryside.

The prospect north-east from near Slievenamon, on a windless evening in August, was certainly as peaceful as one could imagine. It was chilly after showers, and the sticks we had collected were smouldering and smoking damply without giving off much heat, so we sat before our tent in sleeping-bags as we looked back over the whole stretch of country we had travelled that day. We had started from the Blackstairs, and now, camped 800 feet up near Windgap, had no higher ground to break the view across – Mount Leinster, in effortless command of the eastern horizon even at fifty miles' range, seemed linked to us by a particular bond over the plain whose varied greens were beginning to sink into one darker shade as the first lights sprang out.

Earlier, we had walked the quarter-mile over the top of the road through woods to gain an utterly contrasting view to the south. With the sun at that time still filling the air with strong yellow light, the massive confused outlines of the west Waterford mountains – Comeragh, Monavullagh, Knockmealdown – crowded the sky, the intervening Suir valley lost in haze but the purple peaks astonishingly close at hand. I am sure that similar memorable panoramas will greet you if you cross this strip of upland by some other route, or take the lane girdling the eastern flank of Slievenamon itself (which had been our own original plan). Certainly you will not be disappointed if you come the way we came: ride west out of Kilmaganny, cross the Callan–Carrick-on-Suir road, and keep along the foot of the slope for a couple of miles, until a lane back to your left climbs sharply up through grazing land towards coniferous woods on the height above.

Next morning, the Waterford mountains were less dramatic and much more distant in the cooler eastern light, as we dropped down to join the main road from Callan to Clonmel. Quite a busy road, but there is no easy alternative, and as we had eaten only a scrap of breakfast I was glad enough to be on a fast highway to coffee and sandwiches, which we found as soon as we arrived in an airy tearoom overlooking the Main Guard. This merely gastronomic eagerness made, I admit, a base approach to the old town of Clonmel, birthplace of Laurence Sterne, which has a charm at once civic and pastoral. Its favoured site by the lovely Suir is not wasted on it, and its prosperous air does not too much disturb the tranquillity which perhaps earned it the arcadian name of Cluain Meala, 'Honey Meadow'.

Looking at the photograph of Clonmel's Main Guard in Benedict Kiely's *All the Way to Bantry Bay*, whose eighth chapter is devoted to the town and gives many anecdotes of its history, I am struck by the old-fashioned air the picture has, and by how much more up-to-date Clonmel felt when we were there. Kiely's photo, supplied by Bord Failte, has no date: if it were of an English town, one would set it confidently in the early fifties, by the bicycles parked everywhere and the clothes people are wearing and the elaborate gilt lettering that states: COONEY. GROCERY AND SPIRIT STORE. Many Irish towns, however, keep much of that atmosphere: cars and vans predominate over bikes, but there are still many family stores with separate doorways and various shopsigns (I think of

Millstreet, County Cork, where one business did triple duty as auctioneer, licensed victualler and undertaker). Clonmel has taken on a definitely modern prosperity, but without losing an older solidity and charm.

When we came down from our long breakfast, we had a second of anxiety when we found our bicycles gone from where we had left them. They had been moved for a moment, we soon found, by a man cleaning the windows of the shop below: he apologised for having alarmed us. An Englishman happily expatriate here in County Tipperary, he advised us by no means to miss the 'Vee road', the classified road that climbs from Clogheen over the Knockmealdowns to Lismore, situated in the most beautiful stretch of the Blackwater valley. As Dervla Murphy observes in *Wheels within Wheels*, 'the Vee road' (presumably the term simply reflects the shape made by the cutting through which the highway passes) is an unromantic name; but I have no doubt that the views are everything they are said to be. However, we had already made up our minds to cross the hills further to the west in order to ride down the Araglin valley, so we did not take the window-cleaner's friendly advice.

West out of Clonmel, you can follow the Suir on whichever bank you choose. We kept to quiet lanes on the north shore, crossing eventually at the bridge at Newcastle, ten miles out of Clonmel and a couple of miles downstream from where the Suir is joined by its tributary the Tar. We then followed the Tar in turn: the lane runs for two or three miles directly beside the green tree-fringed water, with a flat-topped stone wall between riverbank and road-verge. The Knockmealdowns rise immediately to the south, while over beyond the pastures of the Suir/Tar confluence lie the Galtees. We sat on the wall's broad sunwarmed stones and ate lunch.

Through Goat's Bridge, along lanes at the slope's foot, and then from Clogheen on the Mitchelstown road, we made our way to Ballyporeen. This is a somnolent, valley town, with no mountainous tonic air, and as a market it must some while ago have lost its role to big, thriving Mitchelstown less than ten miles to the west. Here, though, at the corner of the very lane we took up towards the Araglin passes, is a big bright bar called, in big bright plastic letters, THE RONALD REAGAN BAR.

The lane running through unkempt, damp hedgerows dispelled

this anomalous incursion. Then, as we climbed by the side of the stream clear onto the slopes of these sheep- and pine-clad hills, we gained in twenty minutes of hard walking (the road being briefly too steep to ride) the true upland atmosphere: we were linked, no longer to the entanglements of greenery and the weedy slow rivers and the ruminating cows below, but to the bald sheer Galtees across on the far side of the valley. Even though cloud was gathering about them and progressively hiding them from view (it was only the following year, returning to the same spot, that I saw them in all the glory of a clearing evening), and even though it soon came on to rain mistily until the near slopes, too, were blotted out, I could not put from my mind the shape of these mountains, and I still saw them rising on my inner eye as we drifted next morning down the wooded, lost valley of the Araglin towards Fermoy.

From Ballyporeen over to Araglin there are several alternative routes, but since all take tiny lanes over the uninhabited hills, all must have much the same charm. Once you have dropped into the Araglin valley, the road west offers the easiest and most restful cycling: downhill all the way, but never steeply, so you are at leisure to absorb the slowly passing scene. It was misty as we floated down, with a sense of secrecy and enclosure, as thick trees and bushes dripped and dripped onto the softly hissing road. Then, a little before narrow Araglin opens into the wide valley of the famous Munster Blackwater, we glimpsed, up on wooded heights to our right, a grey romantic castle, as remote and graceful and austere as a French chateau I used once to pass, long ago, in the Corrèze. . . . This, I suppose, was Castle Cooke, shown on the OS map. My guidebook tells me nothing about Castle Cooke, whether it is a ruin or a habitable place, whether it was built by early or by late invaders of this valley's peace.

Route 3:
The Glen of Aherlow – Tipperary to Galbally to Tipperary

OS 18 (Tipperary). Distance: approx. 22 miles

Location: The Glen of Aherlow lies 4m S of Tipperary town, between the narrow E-W ridge of Slievenamuck (1,216 feet) and the mass of the Galtees.

Itinerary: This is a circular route from Tipperary town. Take the classified road ESE out of Tipperary, for Mitchelstown via Galbally. At Galbally (11m), turn left on lanes, following the Aherlow river E and keeping where possible on its N bank. At the hamlet of Newtown (17m), take the left fork uphill steeply over the ridge between Slievenamuck and Carrigeenina. At the foot of the slope turn right then left on lanes to Tipperary (22m).

The Glen of Aherlow (pronounced with the stress on the first syllable) brings together in the compass of a single stretch of river valley the elements of pasture, hedgerow, flowing water, dark forest and bare mountain which make up the South Country's landscape. The long ridge of Slievenamuck offers a fine view of the Galtees from the north, a complement to the prospect from above Ballyporeen. I came to Aherlow after a hard day's ride from the north-western shore of Lough Derg and then across the plain of east County Limerick. The Glen is easily included, however, in any itinerary south-west down the Vale of Tipperary, and the route given here, a round trip from Tipperary town, makes a pleasant, easy excursion from there or from Cashel. It is worth cycling in the anti-clockwise direction I have suggested: that way, you are already cycling down the Glen, wondering perhaps (under your breath, as it were) if it deserves *quite* the celebrity it has, before you tackle the stiff push up over Slievenamuck and, looking back and across, understand that indeed it does. The particular quality of this landscape, its tranquillity and its strangely combined sense of being at once open – for you see, to the east, way down the broad vale to Slievenamon – and enclosed, by the sheer mass of the Galtees opposite, is best felt at dawn and dusk. Sleeping the night here as I did, a cold clear night in the fine early September of 1986, I saw both sunset and sunrise. The trees and hedges looming darkly from the pale mist made a farewell image of quiet inland fertility to carry with me on my long ride up to Portarlington station and the ferry home to Britain.

I suppose one should not quote Wordsworth in evocation of a landscape he never saw, but I cannot resist reminding you of these few lines from *Tintern Abbey*, which convey something of Aherlow's delight:

> Once again I see
> These hedgerows, hardly hedgerows, little lines
> Of sportive wood run wild: these pastoral farms,
> Green to the very door: and wreaths of smoke
> Sent up, in silence, from among the trees!
> With some uncertain notice, as might seem
> Of vagrant dwellers in the houseless woods,
> Or of some Hermit's cave, where by his fire
> The Hermit sits alone.

All the sweeter, all the more apt, if you can see yourself, sitting by your campfire, as (temporary) 'Hermit'.

The route is straightforward. Out of Tipperary, keep to the main road to Galbally and Mitchelstown. This road, by no means busy, follows the cutting made by the upper Aherlow River through the western end of Slievenamuck ('Mountain of the Pig'), the spit of high ground which makes the northern rampart of the Glen. In 1987, the long hard haul up Slievenamuck featured in the Irish Milk Race – not the first time that I have gasped my way up a particularly severe gradient to find it figuring subsequently in a bicycle race. Maybe this was one of the climbs that built up Stephen Roche's strength for his remarkable double triumph in the Giro d'Italia and the Tour de France.

At Galbally (pronounced, confusingly, with the stress on the first syllable, which rhymes with 'pal'), turn east into the Glen, and follow the river down, keeping where possible on the north bank. The Galtees rise opposite you, as abrupt here as on their southern flank, clothed with state forests above the fertile dairy farms of the valley.

There are state forests, too, on the slopes of Slievenamuck. If tired or lazy, you can follow the river down to the Caher road and so back to Tipperary without so much as breaking sweat; but if you do push up over Slievenamuck, you will not regret it. Taking a left turn at the hamlet of Newtown, you will find your view obscured at first by trees, but just at the 'elbow' in the road (plainly visible on the OS map), the forestry service has considerately cleared an open space. As well as a car park, there are plain wooden tables set on the grassy slope: simple, attractive, and, when I was there, quite free of litter. There is a superb prospect of the Glen, of the Galtees, and of the Tipperary Vale. Stop here and make a cup of tea or open a bottle of stout.

It was here, indeed, that I camped for the night, having found with some difficulty a flat space almost as large as my tent. Until dusk, I was puzzled, though not unpleasantly disturbed, by regular and very loud reports, as of a gun going off, echoing every twelve minutes or so in the otherwise silent valley. These could hardly be birdscarers, for the country seemed all grazing – unless perhaps there were orchards hidden from view? Most likely, I concluded, this was a device to keep hares from the forests: hares, I seem to recall, are a pest to foresters, nibbling at the saplings until they kill them off.

As the last explosive crack died away, a lady drove up the slope below and stopped at the corner of the road. Here, twelve or fifteen feet high, stands a statuesque Christ: the lady had come up, with the fall of darkness, to switch on the lights illuminating the statue from beneath. Some involuntary Protestant antipathy to images, or a too fastidious aesthetic sense, made me regret this incursion into the pantheistic Glen. It is hard to suppose that Wordsworth, or his Hermit, would understand how that gaudy, sincere idol could deepen rather than disrupt any traveller's reverential mood.

Route 4:
Newport, County Limerick to Templemore – The Silvermines

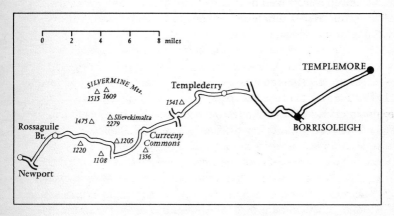

OS 18 (Tipperary). Distance: approx. 38 miles

Location: Newport, County Limerick, is a small scattered settlement some 7m due S of Killaloe at the foot of Lough Derg, lowest of the Shannon lakes. Templemore is 8m N of Thurles in the Tipperary Vale.

Itinerary: From Newport continue E on the Thurles road for about 1m before taking lanes left to Rossaguile Bridge (4m). Follow the Doonane River up beneath Knockfune and then, as the road begins to descend again, take a lane left up over Curreeny Commons to the classified road signposted left to Nenagh. After less than 1m take a lane right to follow the valley of the upper Nenagh River down by lanes to Templederry (22m). Continue E to the main Nenagh–Thurles road, taking this right to Borrisoleigh (30m). Here take the classified road left to Templemore (38m).

According to the OS map, the Silvermine Mountains are, strictly speaking, just the small chain of peaks some ten miles south of Nenagh. However, perhaps because the name is an attractive one, it is sometimes used – and I use it here – to refer to the entire compact group of hills and mountains lying south-east of the lower end of Lough Derg, and separating that lake from the Tipperary Vale.

There are indeed mines in the Silvermines, yielding not just silver but lead and zinc, and worked by a Canadian company under licence from the Irish government. But our road through the hills passed no sign of industry. We had taken one of several possible ways east through this unassuming upland: the Silvermines group is traversed by quite a network of lanes, giving the cyclist scope to pick whatever route most appeals or fits in best with her or his overall plans.

Newport is a loosely defined settlement (don't rely on shopping here) where the Nenagh turning forks north off the main road from Limerick city to Thurles. You might come to Newport after exploring either shore of Lough Derg, or you might come to it as we did after crossing the Limerick plain. Our plan was to camp in the hills, and we rightly foresaw that the lane up the valley of the Doonane River from Rossaguile Bridge would take us into the upland by easy gradients. We managed somehow to lose ourselves among attractive woods just east of Newport itself, but were cheered in our search for the right road by the fine calm late afternoon weather, by the invigorating pine-tree scents, and by the soft gurgling of the streams we kept crossing.

Having no water for the evening, we called in at a cottage just up from Rossaguile Bridge. No doubt we could fill up at some streamlet further on, but perhaps it would be as well to get tap water. . . . The lady of the house took our two containers in through her kitchen window. She was pleased to help us, she explained, but was not sure she had water to fill both of these: she had no tap, but took what she needed from a stream behind the house. . . . We thanked her for her kindness and assured her that we could manage without putting her to any trouble. As we walked smiling out of her front gate, a visitor, a woman with a 'sensible' red bicycle, sturdy and innocent of gears, was coming to call.

The Doonane valley has little dairy farms all along its floor, which lies some way below the road. Beyond, Slievekimalta rises, its lower slopes dark with conifers. At the top of the valley, the lane runs alongside a thicket that grows on the banks of the stream which is all that remains, here, of the Doonane. For the sake of firewood, we pitched camp, Kate scrambling in and out of the thicket until she had gathered wood enough to last all the long evening, while I made tea. The road, like any Irish lane in quiet country, was not exactly busy: I doubt that three cars passed all night. Maybe two hours after we had stopped, however, the woman with the red bike came by, stopping to wish us good evening. She was on her way back, she explained, to her home in Rear Cross. It is cheering to find the bicycle still used (as we ourselves use it) not just for sport or tourism, but for everyday transport – and all the more cheering when the rider, well into her fifties, clearly finds it a pleasure to cycle a return trip of twenty-five miles, with five hundred feet to climb each way, for Sunday afternoon tea with a friend.

Next morning was wet. And ten minutes after we had set off, we had to stop when a tyre – on my rear wheel, of course – punctured. I had been misfortunate with punctures, failing to follow my own good advice and fit new covers before the trip; yesterday had been a Sunday, with all shops shut, and now I had no spare inner tube with me, or none that I could rely on. For once, and in heavy rain too of course, I was going to have to mend a tube beside the road. . . . Off with the panniers, off with the wheel, off with the cover. Kate helped me locate the hole, and then moved away to a safe distance. Impatiently I smeared rubber solution on the wet surface of the inner and applied a patch. Obviously this was never going to work. Either we would have to walk to Templemore, the nearest place likely to have a bike shop, or else Kate would have to ride on ahead, buy a new inner, and then ride back. All very well, but Templemore was about thirty miles off. Work it out: K. cycles to Templemore and back, that's fifty miles, assuming I walk ten miles meanwhile. That's a whole day's ride. And we've barely any food. . . . Yep: hiss, hiss: the patch had lifted off, the repair was useless.

'Look,' said Kate. 'Don't get annoyed, Mart, but what you have to do is *dry* the tube. Please, leave it to me.'

Kate found the tissue paper in her panniers. Sheltering the tube under her cape, she carefully and thoroughly dried all round the hole. Then, while I checked inside the cover and removed the offending thorn (otherwise all that happens is that you get a fresh hole in the same place), she applied a new patch – with firm, gentle pressure, as is her style. Brilliant. It worked, of course.

The rest of the ride, in improving weather, was delightful.

Turning left at a fork, we took the lane high over wild Curreeny Commons, with state forests and bogland and rough grazing, a landscape well fitted to the ragged, clearing sky and strong breeze we now had. At the Nenagh–Tipperary road, we turned left, and then immediately right down the steep-sided valley, almost a ravine, of the Nenagh River. At first the lane rides high on the northern shoulder of the valley, with charming, inaccessible pastures across on the far bank of the stream which rushes through rocks below. Further on – and here I became particularly glad about the successful repair – there is a precipitous, exhilarating descent: only fools let their bikes really go when they are loaded up with gear, but this was fun even with a firm hand on the back brake.

So through mazy lanes to the upper valley of the Clodagh River, a tributary of the Suir which appears to change its name, herabouts, to the Cromoge. We followed its banks down as far as Borrisoleigh. Now breakfast here, since what with our rainy start we had eaten almost nothing, was almost more than we could resist; but on the other hand Templemore, with its rail station, was our goal for the day, and after brief debate we chose to press on for the last ten miles, on a flat straight road, so that once we had stopped (oh luxury!) we need not start again.

Templemore is a grey, long, narrow, serious town, with a pleasantly wide main street, less bustling than Thurles a dozen miles to the south but busy enough to have a hotel and, what we immediately desired, several pubs. We left our bikes in the sun outside one of these and applied ourselves singlemindedly to glasses of stout and toasted cheese sandwiches: after our morning of tribulation and delight, these simple nourishments had the overwhelming force of some hallucinogen, impelling us both into a wordless enchantment. Somehow, after three glasses and three sandwiches, we found the strength of character to seek out a hotel, leave our bikes and gear, bathe, put on 'smart' clothes (not so smart after a fortnight in panniers: this was the last day of our holiday), and return to the pub – a most pleasant place, we had decided.

In Ireland, the pubs stay open all afternoon, and the scene when we reappeared after two hours' absence was all but unchanged: the same eight or ten drinkers, by no means unpleasantly tipsy, still with pints of stout three-fourths drunk in their hands.

We were now able to contemplate a little mild conversation. Were we staying in Templemore, one man asked us, or just passing through?

'We'll be staying here the night,' I replied, 'but tomorrow morning we're catching the nine o'clock train to Dublin.'

'The nine o'clock to Dublin,' said the man reflectively. 'Now I've been trying to catch that train for three days.'

Route 5:
Kenmare to Lough Allua, by the Derrynasaggart Mountains

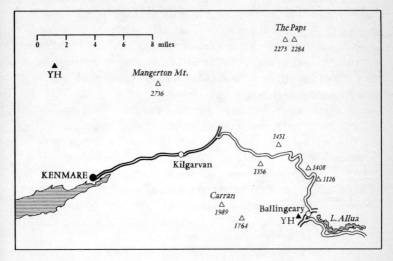

OS 21 (Kerry, Cork) and 24 (West Cork). Distance: approx. 32 miles

Location: Kenmare is at the head of the drowned valley dividing the Beara and Iveragh Peninsulas. Lough Allua is in the uppermost reach of the River Lee, about 7m WSW of Macroom.

Itinerary: From Kenmare, follow the classified road along the N bank of the Roughty River through Kilgarvan (7m). Turn right across the river at Morley's bridge (10m) and follow the upper Roughty until the lane forks. Here take the left fork past the Top of Croom inn (15m). Beyond here take the right fork and follow the contour road until you reach a T-junction with the wide lane (now reclassified as an 'R' road) from Ballyvourney to Inchigeelagh. At this junction (21m), take the right turn and then weave through complex lanes to Ballingeary (Beal Atha an Ghaorthaidh) (27m). Leave Ballingeary on the classified road towards Bantry and the coast, but after crossing a small river just out of town double back left on the lane which follows the S shore of Lough Allua towards Inchigeelagh (32m).

Some of the finest cycling in Kerry and west Cork is to be enjoyed out on the headlands and peninsulas: suffused with the sounds and smells of the Atlantic, bathed in its varying light, these rides belong above all to the sea, and are accordingly described in chapter 6: but they are mountain rides too.

A little way inland, west Cork has more fine scenery – high peaks, empty valleys, clear streams, dark forests. Less celebrated than the tourist highspots of neighbouring Kerry, this area is for that reason less frequented also. You should make a point of visiting it. There are many routes back inland from the Cork and Kerry headlands: across from Tralee through County Limerick to the Silvermines, by way of Killarney and Millstreet, through the Pass of Keimanagh north-east of Bantry. But none could be finer than the route described here, which follows the Roughty River up out of Kenmare and then branches off through the Derrynasaggart Mountains. Apart from its scenic magnificence, a purely inland and upland beauty to contrast with the sea-girt landscapes you have just left, it offers the cyclist the special pleasure of a climb at once impressive and gradual, taking you to over 1,000 feet without once obliging you to get off and push. The view that rewards you at the col is followed, first by exhilarating lanes among wild mountain grazing, and then by a long descent which lets you look back at ease on the heights you have just crossed.

I prepared for the climb by having a lazy breakfast in Kenmare, sunny and cheerful this Sunday morning, still (in late June) much more evidently peopled by local residents than by visitors. Out of Kenmare to Kilgarvan you can follow lanes along the south bank of the Roughty, but these switch up and down among the hills, and in view of the ascent before me I judged it wise to keep to the flat main road, well surfaced and uncrowded. The lower stretch of the Roughty valley is unremarkable, pleasant, with woods on the far side of the river and the slopes of Mangerton Mountain to your left (though the peak is not visible from down here). Kilgarvan is a smallish, straggling village, a pub or two and a shop or two: you may like to note that you can ride here from Bantry, around twenty miles to the south, through what looks on the map (OS 24) to be a wild and austere pass.

Some four miles beyond Kilgarvan, the river swings away to the east, and you leave the main road and take a lane following its gradual ascent. You cross its fifteen-foot rocky gorge just at the lane's junction with the main road, and then climb beside it, stony rapids alternating with more placid levels, all set in a wide valley with mountains on every side. Five miles or so up, the lane forks, and here you bear left, away from the Roughty. (The right fork, staying with the river, peters out into a track further on: but this track, which climbs steeply over the 1,500-foot contour, may well be passable with a bicycle. Here is yet another of the untaken roads which call me back, even as I write, to Ireland.)

Looking back as you near the highest point of the climb – a glance at the map will confirm that you have crossed the 1,000-foot contour – you will be delighted by the wide prospect that opens up as the road twists to give a clear view right back down the valley, across to the tall peaks of Mangerton and, beyond, of MacGilli-cuddy's Reeks, including Carrauntoohil, at 3,414 feet the highest mountain in Ireland. It was here that I stopped to picnic, my Kenmare breakfast all used up. Just beyond, there is an inn, the Top of Croom, which claims plausibly enough to be 'the highest pub in Ireland': on a showery day, you might choose to eat here, though you will not have the pleasure of that memorable view. In any case, this is a ride for a fine or at least a clear day, and certainly not one that I would attempt in really wet weather.

A little beyond the pub, and just over the boundary into County Cork, the lane forks again: the wider road, to the left, continues on directly down to Ballyvourney, in part of the Cork Gaeltacht and near the little village of Coolea which was the home, so my friend Diarmuid Drury tells me, of Sean O'Riorda, known as a great exponent of traditional Irish music. I took the right fork, a narrow but well surfaced lane which keeps more or less on the level, following contours on the side of the mountains and into the heads of valleys. This is some of the loveliest and remotest country I have cycled in. Away to the north now you will see on the horizon the twin peaks of the Paps, each with its nipple-like cairn: easy to understand, from here, how they earned their name.

Still above 1,000 feet, you emerge onto a plateau which for three or four miles offers panoramic views down over the valley of the Lee to the south (the Derrynasaggart range marks the watershed between the Lee and the Blackwater, which now lies over the col behind you). Among the woods and valleys below, you may catch sight of the narrow ribbon of Lough Allua, more a series of pools than a single lake, just below the Lee's source. You drop off the plateau when you come to a T-junction, with a wide and excellently surfaced road leading away down to the valley of the

Sullane River between Ballyvourney and Macroom to your left, or if you fork right, as I did, by lanes towards Lough Allua. The maze of little roads down to Ballingeary is complex, and navigation is made harder both by the fact that the 'join' between the two OS sheets, 21 and 24, comes just here, and by the practice, customary in Gaeltacht areas, of giving place-names only in their Irish form. When you are coasting downhill after a long mountain ride, it is especially tempting, moreover, to freewheel through lane junctions and trust to intuition (luck) where roads fork. . . . But I found Ballingeary (Beal Atha an Ghaorthaidh), so it seemed, without consulting the map and just by taking whichever road led most definitely downhill.

A group of boys crossing the road to the local swimming pool, towels under their arms, confirmed that this was indeed Ballingeary, and one of them added politely: 'Nice bike, mister.' I admit that I too was feeling pleased, not only with the bike but with the rider also. A delightful, unforgettable mountain crossing.

Too bad for the boys' swim, it set in to rain, and I thought I would stay in Ballingeary Youth Hostel. Somehow I managed to miss the turning, but this turned out to be a piece of good fortune, for the shower soon passed and I reverted to my original plan of camping beside Lough Allua. A quiet lane follows the south shore of the lough, climbing in and out among little hillside farms and woods before running for a couple of miles right at the water's edge. I found a pleasant grassy slope with a small pebble beach, and a circle of charred stones to show that I would not be the first – nor, I am sure, the last – to light my fire there.

Route 6:
The Ballaghbeama Gap – Owenreagh Valley to Killorglin

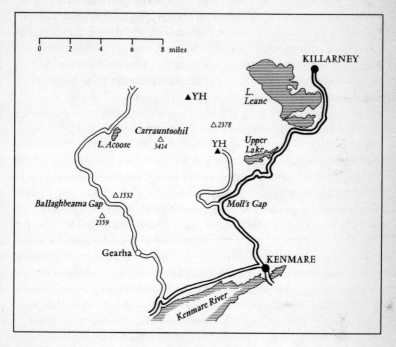

OS 20 (Dingle Bay). Distance: approx. 40 miles

Location: The Owenreagh valley runs W from the uppermost of the Killarney lakes, and lies below the Killarney to Kenmare road. The Ballaghbeama Gap is 5m SW of the highest peaks of MacGillicuddy's Reeks; Killorglin is in low-lying country 7m N of the same peaks.

Itinerary: From the Owenreagh valley, climb to join the classified Killarney–Kenmare road at Moll's Gap, and so down to Kenmare (8m). Ride out along the N shore of Kenmare River to Blackwater Bridge (15m). Here turn right on lanes, keeping E of Blackwater until you cross it at Gearha (20m). Climb on lanes from Gearha via the col of Ballaghbeama Gap to drop down Caragh valley to Bealalaw Bridge (29m). From here there is a choice of routes on lanes to Killorglin (40m).

South out of Killarney on the road to Kenmare and Bantry, you pass through luxuriant woods, damp and warm, before climbing to the vantage-point of Moll's Gap, with views down along the Killarney vale. The road, part of the Ring of Kerry, is crowded, but a turning off to the right will take you onto quiet lanes. This road itself divides after less than a mile: we forked right and dropped steeply towards the Owenreagh River, which together with the Gearhameen just to its north feeds the Killarney lakes. As we began the descent, there was a jolt – I must have ridden over a stone – and a metallic ping!, followed by a regular chafing where the brake-blocks were catching at the rim of my now buckled rear wheel: I had broken a spoke. . . . That could be attended to tomorrow. For the present, we would enjoy our evening.

At dusk, sitting by our fire near the bridge across the Owenreagh, we gazed west to where the sun was going down in a cauldron of mist and light cloud, white and grey and red against the black slopes of MacGillicuddy's Reeks. There was no sound from the few nearby dwellings, and on the road behind us hardly a car passed, although three or four groups of cyclists made their way in the twilight to the Youth Hostel in the next valley.

We had already decided on our route for the next day: out along the Kenmare River – the drowned valley dividing the Beara and Iveragh peninsulas – and up by the Blackwater and Kealduff rivers to the Ballaghbeama Gap. (It is possible to join the Ballaghbeama road by lanes running west from where we were camping, and if one were cycling from Killarney with the whole day before one, this would be the obvious choice. However, since we had to shop – and now, to fix my broken spoke – we would go by way of Kenmare.)

We woke, alas, to the insistent tapping of rain: just one of several occasions, in this record-breakingly damp August, to reflect that the adage about 'red sky at night', not exactly trustworthy in England, is totally unreliable in Ireland. Last evening had been as lovely, in every way, as you could ask for. Still, we had made the most of it. Now we would sit in our tent and look through the *Cork Examiner* (again) and see if perhaps by nine, or ten, it had turned dry so we could cook breakfast. . . . But it was not to be and, after just making a cup of tea in the shelter of the tent, we bundled our damp gear onto the bikes and set off on the steep push back up to Moll's Gap and the Kenmare road.

It is an easy run down to Kenmare, through wild rocky country in contrast to the wooded lushness of Killarney. On a clear day, there would surely be splendid views out along the estuary between the two mountainous headlands. The rub-rub-rub of the buckled wheel was irritating, but I would fix that soon. The rain trickling at our necks was dispiriting, but maybe by lunch the sun would break through. . . . We stopped at a garage on the outskirts of the town. Off with the back wheel, off with the tyre (how maddening, to have to remove a tyre when you haven't even got a puncture).

Now for the dodgy part. There is a special tool – at least I had remembered to bring it with me – whose two teeth fit into holes cut at either side of the freewheel block. Insert teeth in holes, then clamp the body of the tool in a vice (which was why we had had to find a garage), then grip the wheelrim and twist it, hard: the freewheel block, probably locked by rust and grime to the wheel, and tightened by the action of pedalling, is not always willing to be removed. And each time I do this job, I have once again to work out in my head, by conceptual gymnastics, whether you must twist the wheelrim clockwise (wrong) or anticlockwise (right). . . . Watched with tactful but patent interest by three motor mechanics, resting from their own labours, I did it: removed and replaced the broken spoke, adjusted the tension until the wheel was nicely trued. Kate had been standing, meanwhile, at a cautious fifteen yards or so. Well, a triumph! The mechanics invited me to their tin of Swarfega and their washroom, and I luxuriated in hot water and soap, always wanted but seldom available after you have been messing with your machine. . . . Why, though, do punctures and other breakdowns, rare enough in fact, come always in wet weather, when one's patience and resilience are low? And why, oh why, was it still raining now? Perhaps we should struggle back over to Killarney and the nearest train home?

Lunch in Kenmare did little to cheer us up. The town – in Irish, Neidin, 'little nest' – is all pubs and cafés, a cheery place in the right weather, but reminding one today of the bad side of all such resorts, places back home like Dulverton or Alfriston, pretty villages awash on wet days with shoals of despondent holiday-makers eating too many cakes and drinking cup after cup of tea, filling the air with unnatural gloom. If you have work to do, well, you get on with it, rain or no rain. Only vacationers – does it serve them right? – are so cast down, so despondent, just because of wet weather.

We looked around the smoky, steamy, crowded café at the bad paintings on the walls. This was a moment which put things to the test – your own emotional resourcefulness, the idea of Ireland as a place to holiday, the supposed delights of the bicycle, the wisdom of going through this with the person that you love. A decision: we would press on over the Ballaghbeama, even though it was after two o'clock now. We would buy chocolate and peanuts to keep us going. We would even buy food to cook on the gas-stove, although it was plain, looking at the rain sploshing into sheets of water on the grey street, that we would not be camping out tonight. But there would be a hotel or Bed and Breakfast in Killorglin, the other side of the mountains.

Out of Kenmare towards Sneem, Waterville and Valencia Island, the road is flat and well surfaced, running close to the water's edge. The Kenmare River was grey and the mist blocked out the view across to the Beara opposite, but the damp light, the dripping trees standing in fields of long grass between the shore and the highway, had their own rainy charm.

About eight miles out of Kenmare, you come to a small river known, like several others in Ireland, and with the same aptness, as the Blackwater: although the true colour is not so much black as brown, foaming into yellow and white where the soft bogwater tumbles over stones.

Lanes run up on either side of the river. We took the first of these, off to the right just before the bridge. To begin with, you are still in the woods that have been sheltering you (or shading you, if you are in luck) as you ride out from Kenmare, but as you climb away from the estuary these thin out and give way to open grassland. The lane, running up toward the highest mass of peaks in Ireland, takes on a wilder and more upland character, although there are still plenty of houses to be seen.

Even now, we all but despaired when a long burst of heavier rain lashed at us. How would it be at the top of the pass? Was it wise to climb up further on what we could sense already would prove an almost unused route? What if we had a puncture, and had to fix it in a downpour with cold hands? As we exchanged anxious glances wordlessly conveying all this, and as the rain fell more thickly, we passed, providentially, one of the new large churches that may always surprise you up any Irish country road. It was deserted, but the door was open. Even pagans like ourselves might have felt it irreverent to scoff chocolate and nuts in the aisle or among the pews, but there was an upstairs gallery which seemed less holy, and had comfortable seats. Each of us, no doubt, noted secretly that if it kept up like this, we might even *sleep* in here: Kate, after all, had once taken shelter with a friend in a tiny chapel on Elba, only to be woken next morning by a congregation of pious villagers come to do honour to its patron saint on the day of his annual *festa*. . . .

Out on the road again, we soon reached a crossroads beside a primary school. There are in Ireland many such seemingly remote and oddly-sited schools: like the churches, they serve a widely dispersed community, and while not part of any recognisable village, they are convenient for a wide network of scattered farms and hamlets. At this crossroads, you must turn left, and then right shortly afterwards, heading north-west to the settlement of Gearha, where the lane divides after crossing the Kealduff River. The left fork, dwindling to a track, runs off into bog and rock and forest at the craggy head of the Blackwater: like many lanes and tracks hereabouts – there is an extensive network of tiny mountain roads west of Ballaghbeama – this would tempt the explorer on a clear day, with many fine spots, I am sure, to stop and picnic or pitch camp.

The right fork leads up to the Ballaghbeama Gap, and this we took – beneath a perceptibly lightening sky. . . . How charming it can also be, this wild wet weather which Kerry shares with Connemara, with Donegal, with all this western coast: with one breath from the Atlantic, the sky begins to clear, pools of pale blue open in the misty vapour, a first shaft of sun catches on a wet rock high up the side of the valley. Pausing in what was now a steady first-gear climb, we looked back, and although the view was still lost in mist and drizzle, we could feel that the rain would lift. And so it proved: dusk found us sitting by a great fire, our sleeping bags spread in the branches of the hedge above us to dry in the last of the sun. Only the farmer's peaceable black dog, wondering if we had more scraps for him, and the loud gurgle of the rain-swollen stream below the field, broke the golden calm of the evening.

That still lay ahead as we got off the bikes to push the last half-mile to the col. It was here that a car passed us: the only one, as I recall, since we had left Gearha hamlet. An hour's climb, in August, in the most celebrated region of Ireland, and just one car to share the road.

At the top of the pass, the defile grows narrow and rocky, a few trees clinging somehow to the crags above you. Over the gap, the road drops quickly at first, and then swings more gradually through the lovely Caragh valley to Bealalaw Bridge: from here, there are several alternative routes down to Killorglin, as well as a fine-looking lane back between the peaks of Knocknagapple and Knocknacusha into the Inny valley and down to the sea at Ballinskelligs Bay. One more road to be explored, one more reason to return to Kerry.

We kept towards the high ground as we headed north-east to Killorglin, skirting Lough Acoose, a steely and sombre sheet of water fringed by reeds and short grass. A track from by Lough Acoose leads by way of hostels and mountain huts beneath the south-western flank of Carrauntoohil, with a prominent warning notice drawing attention to the perils of these lonely moors. As you follow streams downhill, however, the country grows less bleak, with thick hedges of laurel and rhododendron beside the road. The unfenced land of the upper slopes gives way to more fertile and enclosed pastures, and the farmhouses are more numerous. At one such farm, we stopped to ask if we might put up our tents in the meadow across the road, and whether it would be all right to light a fire. Certainly, the woman said.

5

MOUNTAINS:
the west

✤

Routes 7–11

Route 7:
Clonbur to Westport, via the Sheefry Bridge

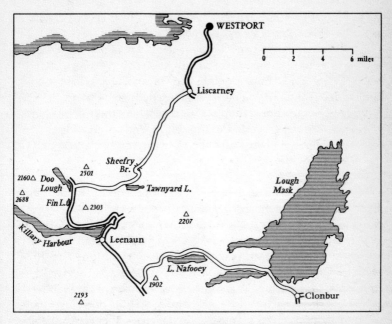

OS 11 (South Mayo). Distance: approx. 45 miles

Location: Clonbur is midway along the stretch of land separating Lough Mask from Lough Corrib. The Sheefry Bridge is in empty mountain country 11m SW of Westport; Westport is at the head of Clew Bay, and lies about 40m NNW of Galway.

Itinerary: Take lanes WNW from Clonbur, passing Lough Nafooey (10m) before dropping into the Maam/Joyce's River valley and riding N to Leenaun (20m). Follow the classified road round the head of Killary Harbour and N past Fin Lough to the Doolough Pass (29m), turning off right on a lane at the foot of the lake to follow the river up past Tawnyard Lough and over the col above the 700-foot contour before dropping steeply to Sheefry Bridge (35m). Ride across open moorland until you reach the classified road, turning left on this for Westport (45m).

Lonely loughs and river valleys, two cols, and the Atlantic winding in a long fjord deep into impressive mountains: this marvellous ride brings together the elements of the Connemara landscape in all their harmonious variety. There will be traffic in summer, especially on the classified road from Leenaun round the head of Killary, but the final stretch up past Tawnyard Lough and across the eastern slopes of the Sheefry Hills is a vividly lonely ride, where you may well not pass a single vehicle.

From a practical point of view, you should note that this is, at the least, a full day's cycling, and you will not reach Westport, which has plenty of shops, until evening. Only the most basic food can be bought at Leenaun. If you have not stocked up beforehand, at Ballinrobe or Headford, shop at Clonbur, where there are a couple of moderate-sized groceries. At Clonbur, too, we were able to cash travellers' cheques at the Post Office, but this might change, and there is no bank there.

Just beside the school and church in Clonbur ('An Fhairche': this is part of the small Gaeltacht area around Lough Mask), the classified road swings southwards: although it is signposted to Leenaun ('Lionan'), you don't take it, but follow instead the lane which heads north-west. You will soon begin to glimpse Lough Mask through trees, and at one point the whole expanse of its shining, island-studded water glitters away to the north (a fuller account of this most exquisite lake, and of the ride down its western shore, is given in route 22). Your road, after crossing the bridge (Ferry Bridge) over the narrow neck of water linking the main body of the lake with the westward stretch that runs below the mountains of Benbeg and Bunnacummeen, follows the Finny River up to Lough Nafooey. Perhaps the monster that supposedly haunts Nafooey is a recent tourist-oriented invention, perhaps – although I doubt it – a more authentic piece of folklore, but in any case this narrow lake, fringed with sand at either end and backed by steep mountains rising on all sides to around 2,000 feet, will live in your memory without need of monstrous embellishments.

Beyond Nafooey (for all its mountainous feel, the lough lies only 94 feet above sea level), the road climbs, sharply enough, to the first of this ride's cols, just some 400 feet high, but with many peaks in view, including the quartzite mass of the Twelve Bens to the west. We passed a group of walkers here, and thought how pleasant walking might be on many of Ireland's empty lanes, which compensate in some measure for the scarcity of marked footpaths. But those heavy backpacks . . . as you swoop downhill, dropping into the Maam valley, the weight of your bicycle and your gear actually speeds you along. . . . Here, in the upper reaches of its justly celebrated valley, the river Maam (or Maum) changes its name, as Irish rivers rather often and confusingly do, becoming the Joyce's River.

This tract of mountainous, river-threaded country west of Loughs Corrib and Mask is known as the Joyce's Country, and the novelist's family, 'like all Irish Joyces' (writes Richard Ellmann in his biography of James Joyce), 'claims descent from the distinguished clan of Galway' whose name it bears. No documents corroborate the claim: all traceable generations of James Joyce's paternal family were Cork people. In spirit, too, this wild empty land is as remote as might be from gregarious 'dear dirty Dublin'. Unlike Yeats, Joyce barely hints, in his work, at the qualities of the Irish countryside, of which he seems even to have a kind of dread: the one real exception to this generalisation is the long story 'The Dead' (in *Dubliners*), a story written in memory of a former admirer of Joyce's lifelong companion Nora Barnacle, who came from Galway.

Dropping down to sea level beside a swift mountain stream, you reach Leenaun (variously spelt, and – as I have heard – variously pronounced). You may be expecting a place of some importance, since it figures on signposts for fifteen miles around, but you will find only a few cottages, half a dozen guesthouses, and a small shop/bar/petrol station. The situation is a memorable one, however, with the fishing boats and mussel frames and seaweed of the inlet leaving you in no doubt that here, among some of the highest mountains in Ireland, you are also on the shore of the Atlantic. Nine miles long, excellently sheltered from the open sea, and with a depth (so we were told) of six fathoms all the way from mouth to head, this is a superb anchorage, and the British used it as such during the First World War. We were told, too – by a man who sat with us by our campfire above Ferry Bridge in August 1987, recalling his childhood and tales of the nineteenth century as well as anecdotes of his twenty years' residence in Bromley, Kent – that the fresh water of the Erriff River, flowing into Killary, remains distinct from the seawater for many miles, and can be dipped into and drunk well out into the estuary.

From Leenaun the road rises to twenty or thirty feet above the shore, before dropping again to sea level where it bridges the river at Aasleagh salmon falls. (At this point, you can take the first and shortest of the three alternative routes from Leenaun to Westport, by way of the lower Erriff valley and then across flattish moors. The third alternative is to keep on the classified road past the Doo Lough and so to the south shore of Clew Bay, where you turn east.) Follow the classified road back along the Killary fjord and up past little, pretty Fin Lough on the tree-fringed Delphi road to the Doo Lough. 'Doo' is an anglicisation of the Irish word for 'black', and there are several loughs so named. This one, certainly, will deserve the title in anything but the bluest weather, for its situation between the high masses of Mweelrea Mountain and the Sheefry Hills, both rising to over 2,500 feet, cuts it off from the sun for most of the day. The main Westport road follows the eastern shore of the lough along all its two miles' length, but you should take the lane off right just past the lough's foot.

To begin with, you follow a river across bog and rough pasture, before climbing steadily past a small, wind-battered forestry plantation. It is well worth getting off the bike, here, and climbing the stile to the marked picnic site in the woods, which gives a fine view down over deserted country past Tawnyard Lough into the Erriff valley. A mile or so further on, at the highest point (700 feet) of the ride, there is another panorama from a heathy, rocky out-crop, with the Sheefry Hills behind you and the level ridge of the Partry Mountains to the east. Now the road drops rapidly, beneath scree-covered slopes, to the Sheefry Bridge, before running across empty bogs to join the classified road half a dozen miles south of Westport.

During this last leg, you will see away to the north-west the distinctive quartzite peak of Croagh Patrick (2,510 feet), the site of one of Ireland's most popular pilgrimages or 'patterns', which you are supposed to accomplish in bare feet – a form of mortification which outraged Thackeray, who gives a full account of the 'pattern' in his *Irish Sketchbook*. Maire MacNeill regards the legends associated with Croagh Patrick as Christian modifications of older, pagan, harvest stories, and she also states, in her long scholarly book *The Festival of Lughnasa*, that there is little record in Irish popular tradition of the best-known legend of all, according to which St Patrick flung down from this mountain all

Ireland's venomous reptiles, thus making of the whole country one great blissful adder-free zone.

Westport, when you come to it – and you will be glad to come to it, for this last flattish stretch of riding takes longer than you might expect – is, as many travel writers have said, an attractive town, with the unusual distinction of having been laid out according to a plan. Such small market centres, even when they lack the modest architectural distinction of Westport, are generally pleasanter than larger but more sprawling and car-ridden places like Tralee or Sligo. The town itself lies some way from the port, which is entirely abandoned so far as commerce goes, and seems never to have flourished greatly from the start: Thackeray noted caustically of the warehouses alongside the pier that they

> might accommodate . . . not only the trade of Westport, but of Manchester too. . . . These dismal mausoleums, as vast as pyramids, are the places where the dead trade of Westport lies buried – a trade that, in its lifetime, probably was about as big as a mouse.

'Vast as pyramids' was surely an exaggeration: and anyhow, times – and tastes – have changed, so that the dereliction of the old warehouses seems more in harmony than the noise and pollution of a modern port might do with the calm of the wide bay on a soft evening. Of course this peace and quiet are no compensation for the commercial failure of the scheme, one of many eighteenth- and nineteenth-century attempts, few of them successful, to stimulate the local economy of the west of Ireland.

Down by the quays lies Westport House, built in the eighteenth century for the Marquis of Sligo. In its ornamental grounds there is a pleasant campsite: it cannot rival the wild places adventurous cyclists will find for themselves among the nearby loughs and hills, but it is green and peaceful, and convenient if after a long day's ride you want to put up your tent within easy walking distance of pubs and restaurants.

Route 8:
Through the Nephin Mountains – Westport, Lough Feeagh and the Belmullet Road

OS 6 (North Mayo) and 11 (South Mayo). Distance: approx. 20 miles

Location: Lough Feeagh lies between mountains just up from the NE corner of Clew Bay. The Belmullet road runs NW from Castlebar (above Lough Mask), across the Nephin peatbog via Bangor Erris to the Mullet and Erris Peninsula.

Itinerary: Leave Westport N on the classified road to Newport (7m). Take the classified road out of Newport towards Achill, but after 1m turn off right on the lane signposted to Furnace Lough. Keep on this lane up past Lough Feeagh to the hamlet of Srahmore (13m), and following it N continue on the forest track into which it degenerates. Push your bike up towards the col. When the track becomes a surfaced lane once more, ride up and then down on this lane to the crossroads on the main Castlebar–Belmullet road (20m).

Apart from the mass of mountains in the Murrisk (the area between Killary Harbour and Clew Bay), the peaks of Mayo lie chiefly in a long chain running inland from Achill Head to culminate in the isolated, unmistakable hemisphere of Ben Nephin, overlooking Lough Cullin (see route 11) and Lough Conn. These mountains, like their neighbours on the south shores of Clew Bay, may well be misty or drizzly when the wind is in the west or south, for they lie directly against the Atlantic. Their grey shapes will be seen wrapped in cloud when inland Mayo, the east shore of Lough Mask for instance, is enjoying drier weather. But they are well worth exploring, and the route described here, the only one in this book which uses rough tracks, takes you right through the heart of them, onto the great desolate bog of north-west Mayo, one of the emptiest regions of Ireland (or indeed, if we exclude Scandinavia, of western Europe). That great bog is described below, in route 16. This present route, while wild and solitary, is less daunting, at any rate in reasonable weather. As well as the pleasure of empty mountains, it offers the delight of the unbroken three miles' ride along Lough Feeagh, whose fine austerity contrasts well with the gentler and more habitable allure of such waters as Lough Mask.

The ride north from Westport to Newport is a little frustrating. You might expect to enjoy a flat run with sea views, whereas in fact the road switchbacks tiringly over hill after small hill, affording not so much as a glimpse of Clew Bay (although numerous lanes off left do run down to the sea's edge). This is drumlin country: as I wrote in chapter 1, it is drumlins, drowned by a post-glacial rise in sea-level, which make up the islands of Clew Bay – of which there are said, implausibly, to be 365, one for each day of the year.

Newport, overawed by an unattractive twentieth-century Romanesque church, is little more than a village: for shopping, it is better to rely on Westport (but don't in any event ride this route without a supply of food, for there are long stretches with virtually no roadside habitation). Fork off right beyond Newport up the lane signposted to Furnace Lough Salmon Research Station. Furnace Lough is an irregularly shaped stretch of water, barely above the reach of the high tide and much favoured not only by salmon but by sea-trout ('white trout' is the more usual Irish name). North of it lies Lough Feeagh, three miles long and a mile wide, and like Lough Nafooey (route 7) having an entirely mountainous feel even though it is not at any great height above sea-level. The Nephin Beg peaks rise beyond it to your left, while to the right a stretch of unfenced boggy pasture, grazed by hardy cattle, slopes up to Buckoogh, not more than an hour's brisk climb and with good views across Clew Bay and out towards Achill Head. Between the lane and the lough's stony beach is a grassy bank with bushes and small trees growing between the rocks, and here and there a level patch big enough for a cyclist's tent.

Towards the northern end of Lough Feeagh the lane passes a fishing pier and a large house, Greenlaur Lodge on the OS map, which appears to be an 'unofficial hostel', for each time I have been there hikers and cyclists have arrived towards evening and walked up its tree-shadowed steps. Above the lakehead is Srahmore, with a modern church whose stained glass is praised by Sean Jennett in his book on *Connacht*. The hamlet is made up of a dozen small farms, and beyond it the lane becomes a rough, stony track after crossing a tributary of the Srahmore River. Here, you are at the foot of a considerable forestry plantation.

The track, passable by landrover and presumably for the use of forestry workers, now climbs gradually, too rough to cycle but not difficult once you get off your bike and push, for the gradients remain moderate (although the going might be rather tough during or after heavy rain). The forest seems neglected, with many dead and dying trees showing brown among the dark green. The conifers do restrict your view, but the track has a fine sense of growing seclusion, and the mountain air is sweet. Then, when the trees thin out and the track becomes a surfaced lane once more, you find yourself in the midst of the Nephin Mountains, with a chain of high peaks running up to the north-west and lonely Bunnaveela Lough just below you.

The lane climbs to 700 feet on the side of Bullanmore, and then drops towards the classified road. Now you are coming down onto the peatbog, and this is an exposed tract of land when the wind comes out of the north-west, as it did when we were there: needing a cup of hot coffee, we found our stove's flame, blown ragged, too feeble to heat water. Eventually we took shelter in the stone-walled ruin of a house and boiled our kettle on a fire of sticks: writing this, I hear again the crackling of the twigs, the wind tearing at the stone walls, and the singing of the kettle, and I see the blue smoke coiling under the overhanging trees before streaming away over the deserted bog. And then on, under a wide, daunting sky, to the crossroads: we could run inland to Crossmolina and so back south-east into the midlands, or we could turn left (see route 16) and press into the teeth of the wind across the bog towards Belmullet.

Route 9:
Under Ben Bulben – Sligo Town to Ballyshannon

OS 7 (Sligo, Leitrim) and 3 (South Donegal). Distance: approx. 28 miles

Location: Ben Bulben rises 6m N of Sligo town. Ballyshannon is in southernmost County Donegal, 4m NE of the popular resort of Bundoran.

Itinerary: Out of Sligo town, take lanes running just E of N, between the classified roads to Bundoran and to Manorhamilton. After crossing (4m) the Drumcliff River, turn left and follow lanes around beneath the Ben Bulben massif until obliged briefly to join the main Bundoran and Donegal road (N15). Once beyond the tip of the mountains, take lanes again, turning right to Ballintrillick (16m). Beyond Ballintrillick turn left at the classified road to Kinlough (23m): as you leave this village take a lane right to Ballyshannon (28m).

> Under bare Ben Bulben's head
> In Drumcliff churchyard Yeats is laid.
> An ancestor was rector there
> Long years ago, a church stands near,
> By the road an ancient cross.
> No marble, no conventional phrase;
> On limestone quarried near the spot
> By his command these words are cut:
> > *Cast a cold eye*
> > *On life, on death.*
> > *Horseman, pass by!*
>
> (W B Yeats, *Under Ben Bulben*)

Drumcliff churchyard – like the Lake Isle of Innisfree, which we later went on to visit (see route 21) – invites literary pilgrimage. Nobody riding north out of Sligo town need make any special detour, however, to see 'bare Ben Bulben's head': the mountain will come to you, there is no need to go to the mountain. It marks the seaward end of the Dartry massif, almost twenty miles long, and paired with a lower and less extensive group of flat-topped peaks, the Rossinver Braes, which lie across the Northern Ireland border in County Fermanagh.

Beneath their curiously flattened tops, these limestone mountains have steep, almost vertical slopes, deeply scored by rainwater
gullies. Their appearance, distinctive certainly, is not straight-
forwardly attractive: Kate went so far as to compare their
crenellations to the ruching of a Victorian pelmet, stately but
absurd. Nor are they tall, even by Ireland's relatively modest
standards (although they contain the highest ground in County
Sligo). However, the impressiveness of the Dartry Mountains, and
especially of Ben Bulben itself, lies less in how it looks from close at
hand than in its dominance of the surrounding country.
Approaching Sligo town from the south, one is prepared to see Ben
Bulben's grey crags, familiar from postcards and photographs,
stretching above the housetops; but what I had not appreciated
until I saw it for myself was how it continues to mark the far
horizon, a darker blur above the blue of Donegal Bay, when one
looks back on a clear day from thirty miles and more to the north,
above Inver or Killybegs (see route 17) on the Glencolumbkille
Peninsula.

The steepness of the Dartry slopes, traversed only by a couple of
valley roads running north out of Manorhamilton (see route 21),
together with the proximity of the Northern Ireland frontier,
pushes into Sligo town almost all through traffic from the Republic
up to Donegal and beyond that to Derry. What with holiday cars
and caravans for resorts like Strandhill, Bundoran and Rosses
Point, this leaves the streets of Sligo choked at busy times: anyone
hoping, as we had hoped, for a sense of Atlantic remoteness and
westerly seclusion had best leave their visit to a bleak November
day.

In Sligo, you may come across evidence of anti-British feeling:
Sinn Fein posters and BRITS OUT painted on walls and road
surfaces. Bigger and busier by far than Donegal town, the terminus
of the Republic's most north-westerly surviving railway line, Sligo
has the feel of a city, although its population is not much over
15,000. However, as the proprietress of our Bed and Breakfast
lamented, here, as in some similar towns (Galway is a case in
point), unplanned and unchecked piecemeal development has
built up a semi-urban sprawl for miles around, dissipating the
compact unity which perhaps made the Sligo of Yeats' time a fine
as well as a lively place.

The main road north to Bundoran, Ballyshannon and Donegal is wide and well surfaced, but busy: rideable if you were in a hurry, but no route to appreciate the changing outlines of the mountains. By turning right off it just as you leave town (we stumbled on a tinker encampment with outrageously aggressive money-demanding children: an unhappy last image of Sligo), you can however join a network of empty lanes that will take you in perfect tranquillity most of the way round under Ben Bulben. First you run due north, through hilly, rushy pastures, to cross the Drumcliff River at the foot of King's Mountain. Passing beneath the jagged purple hills that form a striking feature in the view north from above Lough Arrow (see routes 11 and 20), the lane climbs sharply in one or two places: we got off and pushed. Once you reach the river, with views of the square tower of Drumcliff church across the fields to your left, you follow a contour around the massif. The craggy tops of King's Mountain, grazed by a few sheep which seem to have penetrated somehow to inaccessible crannies from which you would swear they could never return, slip away behind you. And now Ben Bulben, obliged hitherto to share the horizon with neighbouring tops, holds undisputed sway above you, as it will do for several miles as you ride round beneath it.

There is no alternative to the main N15 road for a short stretch a little north of Drumcliff. It takes you over the western limit of the higher ground, and then as it swings down again in a long curve towards the coast at Grange you take lanes again, turning off east along the contour towards Ballintrillick ('Ballaghnatrillick' is the spelling on the OS map: the simplified version figures on the signpost). Beyond there, you have three miles or so to go before reaching the main road to Kinlough, and so along another lane to Ballyshannon.

The ride to Ballintrillick is fine, easy, scenic cycling, everything lovely both in the distant prospects and beside the quiet lanes you follow. County Donegal is in view now: the Blue Stacks and the mountains towards Glencolumbkille float on the horizon beyond the wide Atlantic stretch of Donegal Bay, shimmering when we were there in warm August sunshine. Close at hand, across rushy fields of rough grazing and beyond straggling woods at the foot of the scree slope, rise Ben Bulben, Traskmore, and the cliffs of Eagle's Rock.

Route 10:
The Blue Stacks and The Pullans – Donegal Town to Ballyshannon

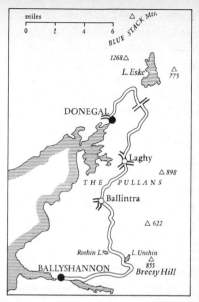

OS 3 (South Donegal).
Distance: approx. 30 miles

Location: Donegal town lies at the head of Donegal Bay, and Lough Eske is 5m NE of the town. The Pullans is the area of small lakes and moorland hills lying NW of lower Lough Erne, and bounded to the S by the Erne River as it flows to the sea via Ballyshannon.

Itinerary: From Donegal, take the classified road for Glenties and Ardara, but look out as you are leaving town for a lane signposted on the right to Lough Eske (5m). After exploring the W shore of the lough, cross the classified Donegal–Ballybofey road and proceed southwards via an exceptionally complex maze of lanes to Laghy (14m). From Laghy proceed to Ballintra (18m) on the former classified road, now replaced by the new highway to the W. At Ballintra return to lanes and ride SE to pass as close as possible beneath Breesy Hill (25m), where the lane swings W and runs down to Ballyshannon (30m).

Eating our picnic lunch in soft, steady rain in Donegal town, where the river Eske flows into its wood-fringed creek and where holiday-makers park their cars, we decided that there was no likely prospect of the weather clearing, after thirty-six wet hours, sufficiently to make it worth heading up into high mountains. To get into the heart of those ridges, running across one after another as far north as Errigal and Muckish Mountain thirty-five miles away, would mean a long ride over to Glenties and then on lanes

north-east. The main road from Donegal to Ballybofey and
Stranorlar does cut through high ground at the Barnesmore Gap,
with 1,500-foot peaks close at hand on either side; but we
suspected, and we confirmed as much later, that this would be a
route too busy to give a sense of mountain wildness.

So we would be leaving County Donegal without having seen its
ridges and cliffs close up, for out towards Glencolumbkille, too,
mist and rain and wind had descended on us (see route 17), just as
we were about to ride up that hard, wild road inland from
Maghera. . . . We agreed on a compromise: we would not turn
south at once, but cycle out to Lough Eske, under the Blue Stacks
Mountains, before swinging down into the Pullans, open moorland dotted with small lakes. We had passed this way as we came
up into Donegal, and while it is hardly true mountain country (its
three 'peaks', shown on the sketch map, barely add up to 2,000 feet
between them), we remembered it as a remote, tranquil upland.
Taking the main road west out of Donegal towards Glenties,
Ardara and Killybegs, you will see, shortly after crossing the Eske
and just as you climb past a petrol station on your left, a lane off
right signposted to Lough Eske. From this turning it is a pleasant,
level ride of about five miles until you reach the lake. Lanes run
right round its shores, and to judge from the map these must give
views of both water and surrounding peaks which would be
delightful in clear weather. From our eyes, however, although it
had stopped raining and was brightening up now, the Blue Stacks
remained obstinately veiled. We rode a mile or two up the wooded
western side of the lough and stopped at a clearing in the forestry
plantation to enjoy a hazy prospect over grey water and past leafy
trees to the island ruins of O'Donnell's Tower, picturesque to the
passer-by but not, I suppose, to the prisoners and hostages of the
powerful O'Donnell clan who were formerly immured there.

South of Lough Eske, across the main Donegal–Ballybofey road
which you can traverse at a number of points, a particularly
complex network of lanes zig-zags through drumlin country. To
find, and stay with, the precise lane you want is, in such
circumstances, something of a navigational test, and we failed it,
spectacularly, returning almost to Donegal town when we had
planned to keep well south of it: the position of the sun, always a
guide if you begin to suspect you have lost your way, was telling me
that we were not *quite* where we had hoped to be. . . . Not many

miles were added to our journey, and in this landscape, which blends the pastoral and the remote as Ireland so often can, anyone would rather look at the views than at the map.

When you do reach Laghy, note that the OS map (1982 edition, roads unrevised since 1976, and still on sale in 1987) does not include a recent road 'improvement', the construction, with a grant from the EEC's Regional Fund, of some new sections of main road between Ballintra and Donegal. I write 'improvement' in quotation marks, since the old road must have been adequate for the traffic it carried – and also because it is an odd thing to find roads subsidised by the EEC (I saw a similar, and quite unnecessary, scheme between Carrigaline and Cork city) while local hospitals and geriatric wards are being closed down, as they were with fierce abandon in Ireland in 1987. Of course, one has only to look across the water to find an entirely similar order of priorities.

Anyway, the cyclist does get some benefit from the new highway, for it leaves the old road to its east more or less empty of traffic between Laghy and Ballintra (which has not done much, needless to say, for the commerce of these two villages).

At Ballintra – vowing to map read more punctiliously, now that we were among mazy lanes again – we turned off left, climbing away from the greener coastal strip into a landscape of rough grass, heather, bog, and small lakes. This is spacious, wide-skied, empty country, with open prospects which broaden as you rise towards higher ground. The scattered lochans bring the daylight, blue or sombre as the weather has it (now, for us, it was clearing to a fine evening), down among the browns, greens and purples of the earth. Towards the end of our journey, climbing past Lough Unshin (charming, but too midge-ridden to camp beside on this calm evening), we had a fine view back: the cloudline had lifted to perhaps 300 feet, and the lower slopes of the Blue Stacks, and also of the mountainous peninsula out to Killybegs and Glencolumbkille, glowed here and there with late sunshine, released at last from their two days of invisibility. But the peaks were still cloudswathed. . . . It was near here that we stopped to talk with two men on horseback, their mounts carrying not only themselves but their pannierfuls of gear. The riders were on holiday, travelling from Donegal town south-west to Clifden in Connemara. They told us they reckoned on covering about twenty-five miles a day, about half what a cyclist will average. And were the horses enjoying the holiday? 'I hope so,' came the reply. I hope so, too, and they seemed happy enough: it is just a figure of speech when one praises one's bicycle as 'steadfast' or 'uncomplaining', but a horse would presumably complain soon enough when it was overtired or hungry.

We camped on open bogland south-west of Breesy Hill (835 feet), with nothing but light airs this blue evening to justify a name doubtless appropriate enough when gales are coming in over the Atlantic. In *The Festival of Lughnasa*, Maire MacNeill records what she regards as a recent survival of the ancient harvest feast of Lughnasa: 'on the second Sunday of July, known as Breesy Sunday, people used to climb to the top of the hill and enjoy themselves with dancing and music'. Though modest in altitude, this is, as MacNeill writes, 'the most conspicuous height in the south of Donegal between Ballyshannon and Lough Erne', and it remains prominent on the northern horizon as you ride along the far shore of Lough Melvin (route 21). Whatever the mythologies surrounding them (and many of the old stories faded from popular memory before modern Irish scholarship set out to record them), the upland places of Ireland still have a charm for travellers which makes it easy to understand why country people would meet on them for solemn or festive gatherings. 'It has been my good fortune,' writes Maire MacNeill,

> to have stood on a few of the heights of Lughnasa. . . . To see . . . the land stretching away on both sides into the far blue haze is to understand how Irish imagination was drawn to roam over wide areas and to embrace the whole country. Most memorable was a fine August day when my husband and I stood on top of Knockfeerina. . . . To know that every year it had been the custom of our ancestors to assemble on these hills in festivity and high spirits, to look out over the plains and pick out the landmarks, is to understand better Irish history, our passion for the wide land, for place-lore, for the itinerary-literature which was one of our predilections.

We had come by Breesy Hill on our way up into Donegal a few days earlier, and had put up our tent a mile or so further along this same road, where we became the object of much friendly curiosity on the part of some local children and their dog. Later, the parents passed in their car, stopping to greet us, and then next morning their eldest boy, seven years old or so, appeared as we drank our after-breakfast coffee: he held out a shy hand and said carefully, 'Here's two nice fresh eggs for your tea.' We stopped at the house to say thank you for this charming kindness, and the boy's mother came to the gate.

'A thousand welcomes and a thousand welcomes,' were her parting words as we rode off. 'It's good to see such nice friendly people up here.'

'Up here': the top of Breesy Hill is just a mile from the Border, and I suppose this keeps tourists, British ones especially, away. Sitting here now on our way back south, we enjoyed a remarkable mountain panorama, with light cloud streaming in from the Atlantic to glow in the sunset as it shrouded the tops of the Dartry massif (Ben Bulben was dominant in the view once more) and of Rossinver Braes over in Fermanagh. The country shows no break or change as Donegal meets the United Kingdom: contemplating the Border in such landscape as this, one can hardly avoid feeling that it is profoundly unnatural in geographical terms, however implacable the cultural antagonisms which make the prospect of a peacefully united Ireland so hard to envisage. We watched a British military helicopter buzz watchfully, now at dusk and again at the next day's dawn, along above the dotted line on the map, keeping surveillance over the forbidden, spiked lanes that run across from the North into the Republic.

An evening of such calm beauty could not but dispel uneasy thoughts, drawing our eyes away from the helicopter to the slopes beyond where the last western light was dying away. Sitting by our fire of thorn branches and scrub willow, we said a regretful farewell to County Donegal, and looked forward to tomorrow morning's run down past the dammed-up waters of Assaroe Lake and the imposing hydroelectric dam at its foot into the compact town of Ballyshannon.

Route 11:
Below the Ox Mountains – Castlebaldwin to Foxford

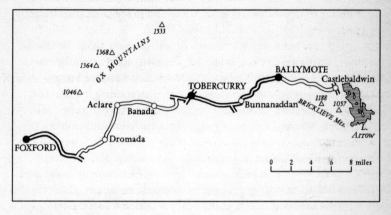

OS 7 (Sligo, Leitrim) and 6 (North Mayo). Distance: approx. 40 miles

Location: Castlebaldwin is immediately W of the N end of Lough Arrow, at a crossroads on the main N4 Sligo road. Foxford is 3m E of the isthmus separating Lough Cullin from Lough Conn in NE county Mayo.

Itinerary: From Castlebaldwin climb by lanes over the N slope of the Bricklieve mountains in a WNW direction to Ballymote (7m). From Ballymote remain on the minor classified road via Bunnanaddan and Tobercurry (18m), turning off on lanes 2m out of Tobercurry to cross the Moy River at Banada and so to Aclare (27m). Turn left at Aclare and head S to the hamlet of Dromada (no nameboard on the road for this village), then head SW to reach the classified road (at 35m) that runs W to Foxford (40m).

This, you may object, is no mountain ride at all – it barely rises above the 400-foot contour, and runs for the most part through lowland country much like that of the midland plain. It is quite true that the lowlying tracts of east Mayo, south-west Sligo and north Roscommon, which this route crosses, are an extension of the plain's carboniferous limestone, and that apart from the climb over the Bricklieve slopes with which this route begins, you will be

traversing a rolling plateau with few noticeable gradients. However, this ride does well illustrate an aspect of Ireland's mountains
on which travellers often comment: the way in which their
compact, well-defined masses rise to the view among the surrounding lowland. In clear weather, you will enjoy prospects back
to Ben Bulben and the hills near Sligo, and then, as you ride west,
tantalising glimpses will appear of the lovely Mayo mountains: the
regular, almost hemispherical curve of Ben Nephin (2,646 feet),
the conical point of Croagh Patrick (2,510 feet) rising abruptly
between the foothills that buttress it, and further to the south the
level ridge of the Partry Mountains on the far shores of Lough
Mask. For much of your journey, too, the north-western horizon
will be bounded by the Ox Mountains (often referred to by their
Irish name, Slieve Gamph), a ridge running from south-west to
north-east and marking for several miles the boundary between
Mayo and Sligo. Seen from just south of Sligo town, these mountains offer a blunt and even gloomy profile, frowning over the bay
and suggesting the great plain of Mayo that lies beyond. On this
route, however, you will find them attractive and sympathetic,
their forested slopes and modest peaks ranged beneath the
afternoon sky. Beyond Tobercurry and Aclare, we drop beneath
their southern limit: if you want a close acquaintance with Slieve
Gamph, you can cross the ridge by any of three cols, and the
middle of these, a lane running up by Easky Lough, is a road that I
have long planned to cycle some day.

It is worth mentioning another point about the present route.
For most of its central section, it follows classified roads, and if you
take it you will have a chance to see not only how quiet these roads
can be, but also how convenient they are if you want to make rapid
progress: their gradients are gentle and their surfaces good, and
they obviate the need for much map reading (an advantage
particularly in wet weather, when repeated exposure to the rain
can reduce your treasured OS ½-inch map to a soggy pudding).
There is, however, an easy alternative to this stretch of classified
roads: from Bunnanaddan, you can take lanes that run more or
less parallel to the route shown, but keep a few miles to its south.

Castlebaldwin is no more really than a hamlet, lying just west of
Lough Arrow on the main Carrick-on-Shannon–Boyle–Sligo road.
The ruins of the castle can be seen. Who 'Baldwin' was I do not

know, although this (like Eyrecourt or Manorhamilton or Edge-worthstown, the latter now renamed Mostrim) must surely be an 'ascendancy' place-name, derived from the family name of the local landowner in days of British rule. From here, you climb the northern flank of the Bricklieve Mountains, which, rising just above 1,000 feet, make the fine backdrop to the wooded islands and promontories and softly shining waters of Lough Arrow as you ride up the east shore of that lovely lake (route 20).

Riding over to Ballymote, you cannot see the lough, but your eye will be caught by the limestone heights above Sligo and Lough Gill, away fifteen miles to the north. In clear weather there is a vivid contrast between the jagged purple hills in the middle distance and the level grey-green table of the Dartry massif beyond.

Westwards out of Ballymote on the Tobercurry road, you pass another ruined fort, built in 1300 by Richard de Burgh (or de Burgo). The Irish held this against Cromwellian forces for four years during the Civil War. Taken by Ireton, it was later dismantled, but its ivy-grown walls are impressive still, dwarfing the local health centre that stands in their shade. You may take the adjacent railway station for another and more recent ruin, but in fact trains for Sligo still stop here.

From now on, the Ox Mountains become a feature of the view – although paradoxically enough they may seem to grow less tall as you near them, for they lack the steep slopes and high peaks to fill a horizon at close range. In this, they contrast with the taller Mayo mountains, impressive both in the foreground and when their blue shapes shimmer on a far skyline. One of those Mayo peaks may catch your eye as far away as here in Ballymote: if you are lucky and have a fairly clear day you can catch a momentary glimpse, as your road rises a little beyond the railway level crossing, of rounded slopes bluely peering over the ridge of the Ox Mountains. This is Ben Nephin, highest peak barring only Mweelrea in all Connacht, and you will see it again from time to time when the perspective of your route allows. After Bunnanaddan, and especially just after the haul up to Powellsborough Crossroads towards Tobercurry, views further south across Mayo will open out, with the peaks of Croagh Patrick and the Partry Mountains visible.

Tobercurry is an attractive, thriving town, with a triangular central *place* giving it (on the warm and sunny afternoon that we

passed through) a pleasantly *al fresco* feeling. Its name, spelt on
the OS map as I have spelt it here, appears on roadsigns as
'Tubbercurry' – a more pronounced Anglicisation of the Irish
'Tobar an Choire'. *Tobar*, a well, is an element in numerous place-
names: not far from Tobercurry are two villages called Ballintober
(on the OS map; 'Ballintubber', again, on roadsigns). Why these
differing usages? Well, I suspect that the Ordnance Survey, who
since early days have had a scholarly concern with Irish place-
name etymologies and spellings, like to preserve Irish forms as
little corrupted as possible in their English guise (this is confirmed
in J H Andrews' *A Paper Landscape*), whereas local people and
local authorities choose the spelling that best captures the usual
spoken pronunciation. All this reflects the paradoxes of the Irish
language in modern Ireland – a language largely abandoned by
the people, but preserved and fostered by government and
officialdom in the name, precisely, of the Irish popular heritage.

Orthography aside, Tobercurry is worth noting as the best place to
shop that you will pass on this route: in 1987 it was the one place
we were able to find red wine (perhaps *that* is why I recall it as
having an *al fresco*, Continental ambience. . . .). It is also the
administrative centre for the North Connacht Farmers agricultural
producers' co-operative, whose fine butter you will probably eat if
you are in these parts. Here, too, is the HQ of the local artificial
insemination service, with a radio aerial on the roof which made
me wonder in what contingency bull's semen might so urgently be
required that a radio message would be necessary to obtain it in
good time.

Beyond Tobercurry, lanes lead off to the small villages of the
upper Moy valley. The Moy runs a circuitous course all round the
southern limits of the Ox Mountains, through Foxford (where it
drains Lough Cullin and Lough Conn), and so to sea at Ballina. Its
westerly tributary, the Deel River which enters Lough Conn near
Crossmolina, drains much of west central Mayo, where the
drumlin belt around Westport blocks off access to nearby Clew
Bay. Little wonder, then, that the Moy is liable to flood, and that
the people of Ballina regularly appeal for better defences to be
built against its sudden rise. This can be rainy country: camped
once beside Lough Cullin, we woke to a downpour which saw the
water gushing in sheets over the smooth sandy shore, and then

rode into Castlebar through floods, on the main road, a good fifteen inches deep: farmers, whole families, were out herding cows to safety from suddenly inundated water-meadows. By lunchtime it was dry (by evening it was gloriously fine), but all that water, held for a moment in the spongy but quickly draining bogs and mountainsides around Ben Nephin, must have found its way to the sea through the Moy River and Ballina town.

It was sunny enough as we made our way through these pretty hamlets of Banada and Aclare, and so down the west bank of the upper Moy to turn off right at the unmarked settlement of Dromada, crossing a lovely stretch of silver-thicketed bogs to reach the main Foxford road. Foxford is an unassuming place with a large, impressive (but not, I think, beautiful) slate-roofed church, a museum dedicated to Michael Davitt, the Fenian and Land League organiser, and a monument to the Argentine Admiral William (or Guillermo) Brown, Foxford's most famous son. A couple of miles on a lane beyond the town will take you to the shores of Lough Cullin, with a wide sandy strand studded with granite rocks and backed by a grassy, wooded foreshore of great charm.

6
THE SEA

Routes 12–17

Route 12:
The South Cork Coast – Ringaskiddy to Union Hall

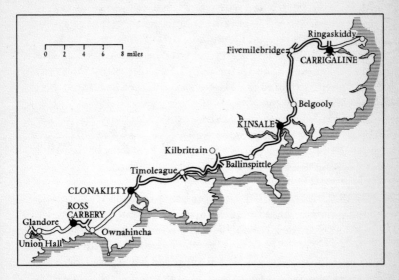

OS 24 (West Cork) and 25 (South Cork). Distance: approx. 50 miles

Location: Ringaskiddy, the embarkation point for the Swansea ferry, is on the W shore of Cork harbour, about an hour's ride out of Cork city. Kinsale is the chief resort of the S Cork coast, and is about 15m almost due S of Cork. Union Hall is a tiny fishing and yachting harbour some 5m W of the larger village of Ross Carbery.

Itinerary: From Ringaskiddy, ride W to the classified road just N of Carrigaline. Cross this road and continue W and then N, on classified roads, turning W again until you come to the crossroads of Fivemilebridge (8m). Here turn left and remain on this classified road through the seaside town of Kinsale (17m), over past Ballinspittle, to the Kilbrittain inlet (but keep S of Kilbrittain town) and to Timoleague (30m). Still on the same road, ride W to Clonakilty (35m), and then via lanes through Castle Freke and Ownahincha on the coast and back up to Ross Carbery (45m). From here ride WSW via Glandore and Glandore Harbour Bridge to Union Hall (50m).

Ireland has a long, indented coastline, and the Atlantic seaboard, broken by innumerable headlands and promontories, bays and inlets, offers the cyclist a wealth of choice. The peninsulas of west Cork (routes 13 to 15) are particularly fine riding, with their juxtaposition of empty mountain and unspoiled shore, but there is much to enjoy in south Cork too. Here are narrow creeks and wider bays, often fringed with woods right to the water's edge, running up into a fertile grazing country whose reddish earth and small hilly fields put you in mind of parts of Normandy and Brittany or of England's West Country. There are some fine sands, and busy market towns (principally Clonakilty and Skibbereen) contrast with yachting resorts such as popular Kinsale and the delightfully quiet harbours of Glandore and Union Hall.

As you ride west, the fields grow smaller, and hedges are increasingly replaced by stone walls, often overgrown by moss and grass and profuse foxgloves and smaller, delicately brilliant wild flowers. Hooded crows rise from the pastures and herons flap over the marshy inlets.

South Cork is a maze of lanes, as befits a prosperous farming country, and it is tricky to pick out a route through their constant forks and branches. Fortunately, this is not necessary. Through traffic keeps inland, and the classified coastal road (the L42 in the 'old' classification) was not at all crowded when I was there in the last week of June: the *Guardian*'s country diarist who rode this way in August also reported that it was quiet, although he was dismayed by the rubbish which had accumulated beside the highway in some places. There may be occasional signs of day-tripping untidiness, but for the most part this road, linking the coastal towns all the way along from Kinsale out through Skull to Streek Head, is a cyclist's dream, well surfaced, easy to follow, and constantly offering new scenic pleasures. As you will see from the accompanying sketch map, this route follows the classified road most of the way, apart from short stretches either side of Ross Carbery.

Coming by ferry from Swansea (on the service which resumed in 1987, with a Polish vessel chartered for the summer), I dis-embarked at the tiny port of Ringaskiddy. This is an hour's ride or so from Cork city, but as I was heading south-west I chose not to visit Cork at all, pressing on instead through Carrigaline and across by the Fivemilebridge crossroads to follow the L42 down by the river Stick to Belgooly and Kinsale.

Below Belgooly, you first meet the characteristic landscape (or seascape) of this coast: a winding, wooded creek which you cross at its head where the estuary narrows, followed by a short but sharp climb over to the next valley and the next town. All the way to Skibbereen you are cycling across the north-south 'grain' of this coastal strip, and there is a fair bit of climbing: indeed, you are as likely to get off and push hereabouts (although none of the hills lasts long) as in the grander but less abrupt scenery further west.

Kinsale lies on a curve of the broad Bandon estuary. It is the chief resort of this stretch of coast, popular with Cork city-dwellers. It has a reputation for seafood and holds an annual gourmet festival: at the checkout of the supermarket where I bought food for my breakfast (the ferry from Swansea gets in at seven in the morning and it was now well after nine), a poster listed the town's seventeen restaurants. If you want plain, not to say stodgy, fare, you can get that too: a take-away stall on the west side of the harbour sold not just fish and chips and sausages and chips, but also potato cakes and chips.

Picknicking in the sun in a little public garden overlooking the yacht moorings, I imbibed all I wanted and more of the seaside atmosphere, for the maritime scent of these muddy harbours at low tide is pervasive and only just pleasant. Yachts are to be seen moored in almost every one of these south Cork inlets. On a sunny day the notion of sailing from one quiet harbour to the next seems idyllic, for the moorings are charmingly secluded. However, all this coast, rocky and studded with promontories, must be a test of skill and coolheadedness when a southerly gale gets up. The race from the Solent to the Fastnet Rock off Mizen Head claims boats, and lives, whenever it is held in rough weather. In Cork, you may momentarily envy the crews of yachts, just as in Carrick-on-Shannon or on the shores of Lough Derg you may wish to be slipping along in a cruiser, but this road that runs so close to the shores of so many creeks and harbours – below Kilbrittain with its sands, up to Timoleague where the ruined abbey looks over the mud-flats, from tiny Glandore across the narrow metal bridge to the yellow, rose and blue terraces of Union Hall – brings the cyclist into as close and silent a relation with the sea as any landlubber could hope for.

Apart from the Abbey at Timoleague, a fourteenth-century

Franciscan friary still used, or at any rate used until very recently, as a local burial-place (some gravestones date from the mid-1970s), the most celebrated religious site you pass is the Marian grotto at Ballinspittle. There are many such grottoes in Ireland, shrines to the Virgin built where a hollow by the road offers a suitable site, but the one at Ballinspittle achieved special fame, or notoriety, in the summer of 1985, when some teenagers claimed to have seen the statue move. A little later, three young children said that they had also heard it – or her – speak, delivering the message: God is angry with the world. In no time, Ballinspittle rivalled Knock as the goal of pilgrimages: we saw a coach trip advertised from Templemore (see route 4), with candlelit devotions on arrival. 'In County Cork,' as Anthony Cronin noted sardonically in that August's *Irish Times*, 'there is a statue of the Blessed Virgin which is said to move. Thousands stand nightly in the endemic rain to peer at it.'

Two years later, not much evidence remained of this temporary celebrity, for the Church hierarchy never endorsed the visionaries' credulity. There is a newly built public toilet, and a placard recording the statue's history, but with no mention either of the visions or of the attack which vandals subsequently made on the icon (although it is stated that the image was briefly removed 'to repair damage'). I must confess to a certain sympathy with whoever found themselves so enraged or depressed by the Ballinspittle devotions that they were moved to damage the statue. It was British intolerance and oppression which made Catholicism an integral part of Ireland's identity, but I hope a Brit can express his agreement with Anthony Cronin's doubts as to whether passive Catholic conservatism can preserve that identity into the era of *Dallas* and drive-in hamburger joints (Europe's first, noted Cronin, had just opened in Terenure, Dublin), or prove any defence against 'the godless contemporary world, its extortionate and uncontrollable economics, its soulless spirit of enterprise, its willingness to contemplate the final holocaust.'

Not that Britain lacks irrationalisms of its own. Returning from our 1985 trip, we came across groups of soldiers all dressed up in camouflage gear near the little station in the Ouse valley near our home. They were earnestly playing that autumn's Home Defence game – pretending to stop the invading Russians at Southease Bridge, acting out their role in rounding up local 'subversives' like me and Kate, or perhaps practising some post-nuclear fantasy of the kind defined long ago by Bob Dylan: 'I dreamed the only person left alive after the war was *me*.' This charade, unlike the one at Ballinspittle, was not just tolerated but organised by the State.

Beyond Ballinspittle lies Kilbrittain bay, a great expanse of sand drying at low tide, a marvellous place for children to run and paddle. Even I was tempted to dismount and explore the beach, but resisted, or rather succumbed to the greater and continuous temptation to stay on my bicycle.

That night, camping among grass-grown dunes just east of the tiny resort of Ownahincha, I did get my feet sandy (but not wet), walking along the beach in the late June evening and enjoying the view away to the west, with cliffs and rocky islets stretching greyly into a grey sea. And so next morning, in fitful rain and silvery misty light, through Ross Carbery and on lanes through Glandore and Union Hall, to a fine picnic site in forestry woods overlooking the long winding inlet of Castle Haven, where trees have been thoughtfully pruned to give a view across the silent bay. There below me a solitary canoeist paddled back and forth in the shimmering, tree-fringed water.

Route 13:
Mizen Head and Sheep's Head – Skull to Kilcrohane

OS 24 (West Cork). Distance: approx. 42 miles

Location: Mizen Head is the most southerly of the five peninsulas that run out into the Atlantic in SW Ireland. Sheep's Head, to its north and separated from it by Dunmanus Bay, is the narrowest and shortest of the five. Skull is on the S coast of Mizen Head, about 14m NE of the Head itself. Kilcrohane is a hamlet approximately halfway along the S coast of Sheep's Head.

Itinerary: From Skull, take the classified road SW through Toormore and along the N shore of Crook Haven (14m) before continuing on lanes W and then N past the caravan camp at Barley Cove. Continue on lanes N of the peak of Knocknamaddree to rejoin the classified road past the hamlet of Dunmanus (26m). Follow this road NE to Durrus (34m), and then take lanes left, keeping as close as possible to the water's edge, and so past Ahakista to Kilcrohane (42m).

Mizen Head, Sheep's Head and the Beara Peninsula are favourite cycle-touring country. Exhilarating mountain rides contrast with level stretches beside the sea: the views from headland to headland are glorious: accommodation is plentiful at the side of the larger roads (half the guesthouses seem to be called 'Bay View House'), but by British or Continental standards the area is for the most part remarkably undeveloped. Traffic is rarely heavy, and on the lanes towards the seaward ends of the peninsulas you will scarcely meet a car. I do, however, remember passing two cyclists, who had stopped to enjoy the magnificent prospect from Mizen Head, across intervening Dunmanus Bay and the hills of Sheep's Head, to the mountains of the Beara beyond. I slowed down to greet them and we smiled in wordless appreciation of the scenery, the clear air and the bright sun: that day, it seemed an image of a cyclist's paradise.

You may well wish to do as I did and cycle all or part of the way along first one and then the next of these headlands. This and the following two routes form a continuous sequence (as you will see

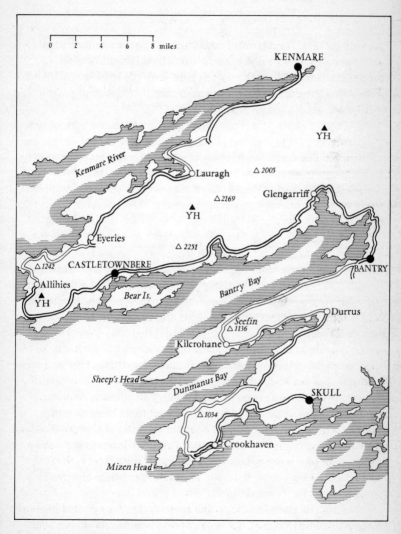

Routes 13, 14 and 15

from the accompanying map); I have, however, broken the ride
into three stretches of manageable length, each of which would
make about a day's ride for the average cyclist.

Skull ('An Scoil'), as it is spelt on the OS map, or Schull as the
roadsigns understandably prefer to have it, is an attractive little
yacht harbour. There are boat trips in good weather to the
archipelago of Clear Island, Sherkin Island and their neighbours: I
do not know if bicycles can be taken, but in any case they would be
of limited use, since neither of the inhabited islands is much over
three miles long. There is a Youth Hostel on Clear Island, which is
a breeding ground of sea-birds and a favourite holiday venue for
ornithologists and naturalists.

West out of Skull, you cross rough country backed by the slopes
of Mount Gabriel (1,339 feet) before rejoining the coast at
Toormore. The finest stretch of this southern coast comes as you
reach the narrow inlet of Crook Haven, with a charming view
across the enclosed waters to the terraced cottages of Crookhaven
town. Perched on a spit of rocky ground between the haven and the
open sea, with the Fastnet Rock visible in spray-veiled splendour
seven miles offshore, Crookhaven seemed a romantically maritime
place on this fine morning, clearing rapidly after early mist and
drizzle: it would be another matter on a lowering November
evening with rain in the westerly gales. The classified road runs
out to the town, and there stops: I took lanes west, past the modest
and unobtrusive caravan site and the splendid dunes and sands of
Barley Cove.

Skirting the steep slopes of Knocknamaddree (1,034 feet), you
find yourself between sea and mountain: a pleasure to be had in
Connemara, too, in Mayo and Donegal and Wicklow, but a
pleasure which these west Cork and Kerry headlands offer in
generous abundance. The bleat of sheep and the song of a lark
mingle with the cry of gulls, and the rustling of the streams which
flow under or across your road loses itself in the beating of the sea
below. There is some climbing hereabouts, with the road rising
above 500 feet where the ground falls precipitously to the rocky
shore below: the reward of your effort is that fine view north to the
Beara over Dunmanus Bay. Back east from Knocknamaddree, past
a ruined castle ('yet another stronghold of the O'Mahony's', says
the Blue Guide), you run for the most part across flatter but

deserted land: neither fishing nor other industry has established itself, although I did see a signpost directing me to the house of a local craftswomen who made hand-knitted pullovers – and another directing me to the consulting-room of a chiropractor. There are small farms here and there, but the land is poor, and you can see across the waters of the bay that Sheep's Head is likewise sparsely inhabited.

If you did not buy food before leaving Skull, make sure to shop at Durrus, which though a tiny place does have a butcher and two grocery stores. West from here, a narrow unfrequented lane runs for miles at the sea's edge, with wide views out into the open water beyond the bay – leisurely, contemplative riding (unless you meet a headwind from the west. . . .). At Ahakista, you plunge into the shade of dense-leaved trees, the road beneath them glistening still, when I passed, with morning drizzle long since dried by the sun from the open lanes. Where trees do grow in sheltered spots on these headlands, they seem to prosper luxuriantly: Ahakista is no more than a hint of what you will find at Lauragh on the Beara Peninsula. I now began freewheeling down dead-end lanes to the shore, looking for somewhere to pitch my tent, and found at Kilcrohane a fine bank of sand and shingle separating a small lake from the open water of the bay. Swans floated on the lake, and beyond its patch of bright water rose Seefin (1,136 feet) in slopes of delicately varied green – straw-yellow where hay had been newly taken, lush and dark where grass stood waiting to be cut, and pale, shining like all these grassy mountainsides of Cork and Kerry, on the rougher pastures above, where sheep sparkled like flecks of quartz among the rocky outcrops. Turning away from the mountain and the small farms and cottages standing among sheltering tree-belts on its flank, I enjoyed an equally memorable view out to the west, where the steep northern shores of Mizen Head plunged into the soft, hazy Atlantic.

Route 14:
Kilcrohane to Castletownbere – The Shores of Bantry Bay

OS 24 (West Cork). Distance: approx. 48 miles

Location: For Kilcrohane and Sheep's Head, see previous route. Bantry lies at the SE head of Bantry Bay, which separates Sheep's Head from the Beara Peninsula to its N. Castletownbere, the most important town on the Beara, is on the S shore of the headland about 12m E of its seaward end.

Itinerary: From Kilcrohane take the lane climbing N over the ridge, passing just W of the peak of Seefin. Continue E along this lane to the classified road (turn left) just outside Bantry (15m). Between Bantry and Glengarriff (27m), you will have to follow the classified road. At Glengarriff take the minor classified road signposted left to Castletown-bere, following this along the S shore of the Beara through Adrigole (36m) to Castletownbere (45m).

Waking at sunrise, I peered out of my tent to see a grey morning, dry but ominously still, with complex layers of cloud lying in pearly light above sea and mountains. I should have got up and struck camp; waking again after another hour's sleep, I found that it had begun to rain, and as I climbed over the stiff pass below Seefin it was coming down in sheets, although later the rain slackened and I had, today and the next day, 'soft rain' of the kind which is so frequent on these headlands. Thackeray appreciated both the splendour of the scenery and the compensations which west Cork's mist and drizzle offer to the traveller:

> We had only opportunity to see a part of the astonishing beauty of the country. What sends picturesque tourists to the Rhine and Saxon Switzerland? Within five miles round the pretty inn of Glengarriff there is a country of the magnificence of which no pen can give an idea. . . .
>
> The day did not clear up sufficiently to allow me to make any long excursion about the place, or indeed to see a very wide prospect round about it: at a few hundred yards, most of the objects were enveloped in mist; but even this, for a lover of the picturesque, had its beautiful effect, for you saw the hills in the foreground pretty

clear, and covered with their wonderful green, while immediately behind them rose an immense blue mass of mist and mountain. . . .

Above Kilcrohane, a couple of dead-end farm-tracks lead inland, but you must look for a wider and better surfaced (though quite deserted) road which leads up in zig-zags to cross the 600-foot contour below Seefin. The stiffness of the climb, compelling me to get off and push, and the extraordinary warmth and humidity of the weather, forced me to stop and take off my tracksuit, so that under the pouring rain, beneath my invaluable cape and water-proof safety helmet, I was wearing nothing but shorts and T-shirt. Still I sweated heavily: at the top of this wild pass, there is a large religious statue, a *mater dolorosa* with the dead Christ in her arms, and I confess I had to repress blasphemous analogies between his plight and my own.

Dropping down from the col, the visibility was still enough for me to make out, across the grey water of Bantry Bay, the lower slopes of the Caha and Slieve Miskish Mountains and the looming form of Bear Island which provides shelter for the fine natural harbour of Castletownbere. The Goat's Path, as the lane running along the north shore of Sheep's Head is called, is a superb, lonely ride, with rocky slopes above and the bay below. As you approach Bantry, you run through a pleasant farming country among small hills, with Whiddy Island out to sea: formerly an oil terminal, this was closed following a serious accident several years ago, and now presents an incongruous picture of industrial dereliction amidst this remote stretch of water.

Bantry huddled in the rain beneath its mountain background, a busy town with pubs and cafés: leaving my bike in a desultory open-air market, I ate a huge breakfast before pressing on along the wide Glengarriff road. This is a tourist route (although it was not too busy when I was there), and Glengarriff – where I stopped at another café – is a touristic village, with boat-trips to the famous Italian Gardens on Garnish Island. Wet as it may be, this is a very mild climate, with midwinter temperatures high enough for sub-tropical plants to thrive.

Turning onto a narrower and quieter classified road, you ride out towards Castletownbere, passing in the first few miles of your journey through foothills of the Caha Mountains. With many peaks reaching to 2,000 feet or thereabouts, the Beara is a truly mountainous peninsula, and as I passed small loughs, encircled by rocky slopes and swept by drizzling cloud, I might have been miles inland in some upland moor. Only beyond wooded Adrigole does the road descend permanently onto the flat coastal strip. Now, as I neared Castletownbere, the westering sun seemed on the point of breaking through, and for a brief moment pools of faint blue opened in the cloud above me. At once the sky, the misty air, and the motionless breadth of Bear Haven began to glisten with intense silvery luminescence, an effect of light so beautiful that I could not wish for clearer weather. At Dinish Island, I cycled down to the shore to watch the Bear Island ferry put out, past a wreck which had come to grief a couple of years previously in the apparently placid, but no doubt rock-strewn, waters of the sound. In Castletown I saw a still more ramshackle ferry, a fishing boat with a makeshift pontoon lashed to its side: after much roaring of the engine, the skipper succeeded in dragging the pontoon from its slipway, and made out across the water with two cars alongside.

Castletownbere is a marvellous place, a fishing-port at once remote and busy, with its one street of houses giving directly onto quays where vans and lorries park to take the catch to fishmongers in Cork and Dublin, for export to France, or to be processed at Killybegs way up in County Donegal. I found a Bed and Breakfast in the heart of the little town, attached to a butcher's shop (my bicycle spent the night beneath a side of pork) whose charming proprietor had the gentle manner more conventionally associated with a nurse or a librarian. Would I want to make an early start tomorrow? – that was his only worry. 'Well,' I said, 'not too early.' 'Would ten, or half past ten, be soon enough for breakfast, then?', he suggested. Out here they make the most of the long summer nights, and commerce next morning does not start until an hour which seems delightfully (or scandalously) late if you come from a nation of shopkeepers.

Just opposite my B and B was one of those Irish bars whose front room doubles as a general store, selling such articles as peardrops and shoe-laces. Here I spent a grand evening: it was Friday, and as the night went on more and more drinkers crowded in, until there was a closeness of physical contact unimaginable in most English pubs. There was singing too, although it was not that elusive, authentic Irish music which you may hear of but which you will not necessarily find: two young women had brought guitars and accompanied themselves in a mixture of half-traditional folksongs

(English, or Liverpudlian, rather than Irish) and more recent ballads. Then a man got up and sang 'The Boys of the Old Brigade', a celebration of the Easter Rising and of the 'old IRA'. I do not think the singer knew he had an Englishman next to him, and in any case I was well aware that by singing such a song an Irish person need not be expressing hostility to a travelling Brit or support for the Provisional IRA of the 1980s. However, I could sense the unease and embarrassment of the landlady and her daughter, who had made me warmly welcome early in the evening, handing me with the compliments of the house a second glass of Murphy's stout just as I was finishing my first, and assuring me that cycling was the only way to see the lovely country hereabouts. The moment passed and the singing, and drinking, went on. Around midnight, I left, to get back to my B and B before they closed the door: I had no key either to this front door (shut with a bolt) or to my room, both of which were left open until twelve, since, I was assured, 'no-one but the family will be coming in and out.'

I was shown into the soft night by a side passage, as the bar was ostensibly closed now – in case, I suppose, the Gardai should happen to pass this way, and should choose (which seemed still more unlikely) to interfere with the Friday night conviviality.

Route 15:
Castletownbere to Kenmare –
The Beara Peninsula

OS 24 (West Cork) and either 20 (Dingle Bay) or 21 (Cork, Kerry).
Distance: approx. 50 miles

Location: For Castletownbere, see previous route. Kenmare is at the head
of the Kenmare River, the drowned valley which divides the Beara
Peninsula from the Iveragh Peninsula to its N.

Itinerary: From Castletownbere, take the classified road W along the
shore, and then, leaving the Dursey Head turning to your left, swing N into
Allihies (14m). Proceed N and then E on lanes until you rejoin the
classified road just before Eyeries (24m). Follow this via Ardgroom to
Lauragh (36m), where you take a lane left past Derreen House to the E
shore of Kilmakilloge Harbour (38m). Follow this lane round the
headland until it rejoins the classified road, which you take left to
Kenmare (50m).

Like Mizen Head and Sheep's Head, the Beara culminates in a
seaward point accessible only by a dead-end lane. Had the mist
lifted, perhaps I would have pressed on out to remote Dursey Head
– even to offshore Dursey Island, by cable-car across the steep-
sided sound. Had the mist lifted . . . I could not agree with the
German cyclist I met towards lunchtime at Allihies, who told me
that she was about to stop riding for the day because it was
'impossible to see anything'; but I was frustrated to find everything
still veiled at midday in shining but impenetrable cloud. Thackeray is right to acknowledge the 'beautiful effect' which this has on
the scenery close at hand, and there is a particular pleasure in
moving in a cyclist's silent, regular rhythm through a little world,
fifty yards in diameter, which changes constantly as you ride; but
on such roads as this, which command glorious views in all
directions, it is sad to record that 'I had only opportunity to see a
part of the astonishing beauty of the country.'

The Beara, as I have said, is the most mountainous of the three
headlands that I explored. If you want the thrill, and the
subsequent self-satisfaction, of a climb both high and hard, you

can cross its spine of rocky peaks by the 1,084-foot Healy Pass above Adrigole, a little back inland from Castletownbere. The way I went is just as remote, and almost as mountainous in feel: the lane winds beyond Allihies and under the Slieve Miskish hills and north of the peak of Knocknagallaun (1,242 feet), clinging precariously and tenaciously to the sheer seaward-plunging slopes. From Eyeries – an attractive village of plain, weather-beaten terraces, looking almost out of place in the empty landscape – on through Ardgroom to Lauragh, I could sense the mass of high ground to my right, and when for half an hour the sky lightened as I rode easily over the coastal strip, the sun gleamed on the lower slopes as they loomed impressively through the mist.

At Lauragh, there are Bed and Breakfast places, and a Youth Hostel where a lane runs up past Glanmore Lake into the mountains (another Youth Hostel, at Allihies, has a similarly off-the-beaten-track setting). There must be shops, too, in Lauragh, but I could not see them: I was glad that I had bought food at Castletownbere, the only sizeable place (population 800!) on the Beara, and I would advise you to do the same.

Oaks and other deciduous trees grow thickly around Lauragh. The sheltered harbour of Kilmakilloge offers a mild and favourable environment – almost too damply warm, you may think, for the trees are festooned with moss, and moss grows everywhere on the rocks and beside the pools and streamlets beneath their dense leaves. Derreen House, whose grounds contain much fine wood-land, is open to the public on some summer afternoons. I found the woods almost overpoweringly luxuriant, and rode with relief out of their humid shade back into cooler coastal air. Kilmakilloge provides moorings for flat-bottomed day-boats, although not, so far as I saw, for larger craft. The entrance to the bay is between rocky, barren promontories, and on the eastern shore I put up my tent, on a spit of land planted with grass and threaded with carefully made paths. A small drystone hut, with unglazed windows and a charred fireplace against one wall, offered shelter: I could have slept in there, and was happy to set up my stove on the wooden bench and cook my supper out of the wind. I do not know under whose auspices this hut had been provided: in Ireland, such simple but welcome amenities are not usually accompanied by any officious noticeboard, disfiguring the site and telling you what you may and may not do there.

After eating, I sat outside, gazing west into sea-spray and fine rain, hunched under my cape and leaning into the freshening wind. The air was clearing, but night was coming on, veiling the surrounding peaks in darkness just as they cast off their last shrouds of mist and cloud. A memorable, lonely evening.

As I had hoped and thought it would, the night wind blew the air clear, and I woke to a bright morning with a wide view across the Kenmare River to the Iveragh peaks out west above Waterville. One day I shall ride out along the Iveragh (which we crossed when we climbed to the Ballaghbeama Gap: see route 6). One day, too, I shall ride along its neighbour, the Dingle Peninsula, last and most northerly of the five headlands of south-west Ireland.

Route 16:
Belmullet – The Bog of North-West Mayo and the Mullet and Erris Peninsula

OS 6 (North Mayo). Distance: approx. 30 miles

Location: For the start of this route, see route 8; the route can also be joined near its start by riding WNW from Crossmolina at the head of Lough Conn. The Mullet and Erris Peninsula forms the most north-westerly part of County Mayo, and is joined to the mainland by the narrow isthmus on which Belmullet stands.

Itinerary: From the crossroads below the Nephin Beg range, turn left on the classified road and continue NW to Bellacorrick (7m) and Bangor Erris (15m). Detour via the W side of Carrowmore Lake to Barnatra, and then left on the classified coast road to Belmullet (30m).

I have described at the end of route 8 (see chapter 5) how Kate and I came down from the Nephin Beg Mountains onto the great plain of north-west Mayo, and how at the crossroads on the Belmullet road we had to choose whether to cycle out to the Mullet and Erris Peninsula, or whether to turn sensibly with the wind and run inland to the central lowlands and so towards Dublin and home. For a moment, prudence prevailed, and we rode inland towards Crossmolina, but after less than a mile we both stopped: both of us had invested the idea of Belmullet with an obscure but intense emotional significance: now that we were within half a day's ride of it, we found that we could not forego the opportunity of visiting that remote north-western outpost. The better-known coastal roads of Connemara offer scope for many rides that would probably prove easier and pleasanter (one day we will return to Connemara and explore its sandy bays and rocky promontories), but this ride, in many ways daunting and gloomy, is worth making if you have a taste for empty, desolate country.

In the first chapter of *The Return of the Native*, Hardy reflects on the modern attraction, already gaining ground in the late nineteenth century, towards sombre and haggard landscapes, 'the chastened sublimity of a moor, a sea, or a mountain'. He contrasts such melancholy and austere beauty with sunnier and more fertile classical ideals, and suggests that 'the new Vale of Tempe may be a gaunt waste in Thule.' 'Thule' denotes an icy, northern region, rather than an Atlantic seaboard, but north-west Mayo might well be called a 'gaunt waste', even though its bogs yield useful turf. You need only look at the map to see how Belmullet, away on its isthmus almost thirty miles from the next sizeable town, might draw a romantically inclined cyclist to set off into the wind and explore the port and the strangely-shaped, sea-worn headland that lies beyond it. This site at the limit of wild Mayo, together with that fine, sea-sounding name, were no doubt what led Seamus Heaney to include the town in the litany which concludes his poem *Shoreline*:

> Strangford, Arklow, Carrickfergus,
> Belmullet and Ventry
> Stay, forgotten like sentries.

So we turned back and made way into the north-wester, a wind that in Connacht seems often to bring clear dry weather (the days of soft rain and low cloud sweep up on humid southerly breezes), but which was tough to fight against as we pushed low gears across the wide and shelterless plain. There are hills away on the northern horizon, and on our left the quartzite peaks of Nephin Beg (2,065 feet) and Corslieve (1,785 feet) loomed greyly, but the great bog itself was broken only by a drainage ditch or a peat cutting here and there. This is blanket- rather than raised-bog, and an exception to the usual rule that only the latter type is mechanically harvested, for the peat is extensive enough and level enough here to repay large-scale exploitation. At Bellacorrick, you will pass a power station where the turf is burned – I say 'will pass', although reports in the Mayo press have suggested that the plant is being considered for closure. Maybe it has closed now, which will be another blow to the depleted local economy: apart from the power station itself, there is employment on the bogs, although this is seasonal and can be precarious – in both 1985 and 1986 persistent rain made the surface too soggy and treacherous for machinery, and Bord na Mona laid off the summer workforce. In autumn 1986, indeed, the bog grew so heavy with water that it began to creep downhill, slowly but perceptibly, until it blocked the road (although this, as I recall, was near Ballycroy, a few miles west of where we rode).

Beyond Bellacorrick, well situated for the prevailing sea-winds, is an experimental electricity-generating windmill, one possible answer to the question of how Ireland will replace its dwindling turf-bogs. Then comes the one green and pastoral stretch of this long moorland ride, as the road follows the valley of the Owenmore River, with small fields and even a few trees, until you come to the dour little quarrying town of Bangor, with a pub and a shop or two and terraces of grey houses and a long bridge across the Owenmore.

From Bangor to Belmullet by the straight road is ten miles or so. We turned off to ride alongside Carrowmore Lake, a yellowish, unappealing stretch of water on this grey day, with hardly a tree to grace its low stony shores. The approach to Carrowmore at the lake's head is pretty, as is the run down to the classified road at Barnatra, but west from here to Belmullet the ride is half-spoiled, despite sea views out to the cliffs of Benwee Head, by straggling houses which are in no coherent or imaginative relation to their environment: here, as on a much larger and more disastrous scale along the Sussex coast near where I live, the buildings seem an intrusion on a landscape that would be memorable without them.

'Forgotten' is Heaney's word for Belmullet, and forgotten and melancholy was how it seemed to us when late on Sunday afternoon we wheeled our bicycles down to the pier and looked across the wide tidal mud-flats. A broken-down fish-lorry was stranded beside piles of rain-bleached wooden crates – as if the fishing had ceased, one afternoon, to pay any longer. And that, over a period of months and years, must be what has happened. Sean Jennett, in 1970, found Belmullet an isolated town, little visited by trippers, but a town which had its market and caught its fish and throve modestly. Ten years later, it was described in the *Cyclists' Touring Club Route Guide* as a 'decayed seaport'. Decay was what we sensed in 1982. Perhaps deep-sea angling trips, for which Belmullet makes a good base, have brought more outsiders to the town, or perhaps (though in the recession of the 1980s this seems hardly likely) some other local enterprise has got going, but it seems more likely that Belmullet will have sunk further into dilapidation. The idea of decay may seem to have some romantic connotation, but having visited Castletownbere and Killybegs, I know that a seaport can be remote, unspoiled, but thriving too.

Route 17:
Donegal, Ardara, and Killybegs

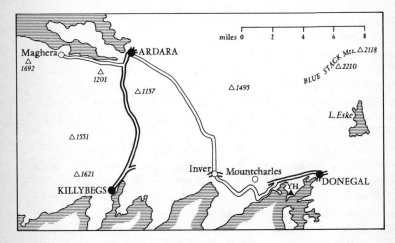

OS 3 (South Donegal). Distance: approx. 46 miles

Location: This route explores part of the peninsula that runs into the sea NW of Donegal town. Ardara is situated at the NE corner of the peninsula; Maghera is some 5m W of it. Killybegs, on the S shore, is due S of Ardara and about 15m W of Donegal town.

Itinerary: Leave Donegal on the main road signposted to Glenties, Ardara and Killybegs. After about 4m, turn left on a lane which skirts the beach at Salt Hill and then climbs back inland: before you reach the main road again, turn left at the crossroads, and then right to follow lanes to Inver (13m). Here take a lane right immediately after crossing the river, then fork left and take a left again, then right at the crossroads to take a lane running over high ground and then descending to Ardara (24m). For Maghera, leave Ardara on the main Killybegs road and take the lane right at Bracky Bridge. Returning from Maghera to Bracky Bridge (34m), turn right on the classified road and so over to Killybegs (46m).

Rounding Ben Bulben north of Sligo town, you will see, on a clear day, the line of mountains west of Donegal running in cloud-capped purple masses out above the blue water of the bay.

We had planned to visit the most celebrated sights of this fine headland, which lie out in the west: the remote valley settlement of Glencolumbkille, the cliffs of Slieve League plunging into the Atlantic from almost 2,000 feet. We had a good ride over to Ardara and camped in quiet, lovely coastal scenery near Maghera. Then a rainy wind came from the south-west: we changed our plans, heading by the shortest route over the moors to the lively port of Killybegs.

The sun shone warmly as we rode out of Donegal, and we turned off through woods to picnic by the sea at Salt Hill. The lane runs at the strand's edge, with views across to dunes, green slopes, and heathery uplands behind. It was low tide when we were there, and the gently breaking waves had withdrawn far to the west, leaving the sun to glitter brilliantly on acres of sand. On this Friday afternoon in August, there were just three other people there.

The climb inland from the beach, over a spit of higher ground, is stiff. Make sure that you pause and turn back as you reach the crossroads: Ben Bulben, invisible down by the seashore, has risen into the horizon, and its dark brow now closes the shimmering prospect across the bay. Dropping down to follow lanes to Inver, you lose this extensive view, but you regain it on the longer, equally stiff climb up to the 600-foot contour below Killin Hill. As well as being quieter than the classified roads to the east and west, this broad and well surfaced lane crosses higher ground, with panoramic views back towards Sligo and the Pullans, west and north over sandy coasts and sea-girt mountains, and away inland to where County Donegal's long ridges rise to innumerable peaks. Near at hand, the country is moor and bog and forest, with here and there a lonely farm set in a patch of rough pasture and sloping hayfield.

The south shore of the peninsula has several towns and villages, linked by a fairly busy road. We were heading for the north shore, which the map shows to be sparsely inhabited. The lane west from Ardara (pronounced, incidentally, with the stress on the final syllable) passes clusters of bungalows before reaching Maghera, with its dozen houses. Beyond this point, the coast is uninhabitably steep and rocky, and the road veers inland up the deserted stream valley of the Owenwee. The whole bay – Loughros Beg Bay – is exquisite, at once wild and pastoral, for below the rocky slopes

that rise almost from the water's edge the narrow coastal strip is
cultivated right to the very sands. At the hamlet of Laconnell,
the anvil-shaped headland whose outline you can discern on the
½-inch map is divided into trim hayfields; and even some of the
little islands cut off at high tide, but accessible by tractor at low
water, are similarly farmed. Patience and labour have made the
most of the soil of this coastal strip, which is broader further north
but which is backed everywhere by bogs and mountains whose
barrenness no amount of ingenuity can redeem. Across Loughros
Beg Bay, whose sands cover rapidly once the tide turns, lie more
coastal farms, their fields of pasture running in parallel strips back
from the shoreline.

Beyond Maghera's salt-marshes, but before the walker's track
sets off round the headland for the sea-caves, tide and current have
built the sand into a mound of lonely grass-grown dunes standing
out in the channel: we tried to push our bikes across to this, but the
going was perilously soft, and we realised besides that we might
find ourselves stuck at high tide – not absolutely cut off, but with
no way back practicable for our machines. So we rode a mile
inland, and camped on a bank above the lane, in the shelter of a
stone wall and a couple of thorn bushes. Here we had superb
views again – out along the bay to the sand-bar, beyond which the
grey Atlantic lay heaving beneath a yellow, windless sunset; inland
to where the sands gave way to tree-bordered mud-flats; back east
to peaks whose names we tried to determine from the map, but
which rose in such profusion, so far into the distance, that we had
to give up the attempt.

Next morning dawned still and overcast: the inland mountains
were alternately veiled and unveiled by low, shifting clouds: it was
plainly setting in for a wet spell. Still, we set off as we had planned,
by way of Maghera for the climb over to Glencolumbkille. We left
our tent pitched and much of our equipment inside it, hoping to
return to the same spot for the evening, and looking forward to an
unencumbered ride. It was not to be: drenching rain began to fall
in the first mile, and with it came a south-west wind, moderate
while the steep slopes sheltered us from its direct force, but
whirling with tumultuous violence down the funnel of the
Owenwee valley. Lashed by rain, forced by the gusty headwinds to
get off and push, knowing that we faced many miles of steep

climbing along an uninhabited road through exposed country, we decided we must turn back – the only time we have ever had to do so. Returning to our tent, we admired the sudden swelling of the torrent which flows beneath the road near Maghera, now gushing in white spate over the rocks before gurgling out into the rain-pocked bay. The dunes whose remoteness had charmed us in yesterday evening's sunset now seemed forbidding and desolate, their sands almost as grey as the steely surrounding sea.

We packed our wet gear and went for sandwiches in Ardara: a gloomy meal. Rain beat on roofs and raced down drainpipes and chattered along gutters. The pub was depressing, with an old, decrepit alcoholic being encouraged to drink by his cronies' admiring comments ('He's not had a day sober since New Year.') One drinker kept using foul language despite the landlord's repeated requests that he should stop; the unsmiling bar staff spoke under their breath to one another and exchanged brief comments in Irish.

The depression of Ardara was soon countered, and vanquished, by other forces and feelings – the fine wild rainy landscape over which we climbed, the good food and charming friendliness which greeted us when we walked dripping and exhilarated and ravenous into Melly's fish bar in Killybegs, the airy comfortable room we found in an excellent Bed and Breakfast, the warm shower and the welcome double bed.

Waking towards seven after a long, hazy doze, I looked out of the skylight and saw that the rain had lightened to the airiest of mists. At the southerly, far-off, seaward limit of the Killybegs inlet, bars of pale green and yellow had broken into the sky's prevailing grey. We strolled down to the harbour, where the final day of a sea-angling festival was ending in the messy, excited business of weighing the catch. Crowded into the quayside warehouse were competitors from Italy and France, spectators from Japan: the barn-like, salty, scaly place echoed to polyglot talk and laughter. Outside, four big trawlers were tied up: alongside the predictably, if stirringly, christened *Atlantic Challenger*, we noted two boats with names more ecclesiastical and Irish (although they might be paralleled in the similar and similarly Catholic ports of Brittany) – the *Paraclete* and the *Father MacKie*.

The soft evening light, the grey-green shores lying beyond

stretches of calm water, and the contrast between this tranquillity and the pleasant bustle of the quayside (there was even a three-ride funfair in Killybegs this Saturday night) reminded me of Castletownbere, and I recalled that it was to this Donegal harbour that the Cork fishermen sent some of their catch to be processed. Linked by commerce and by their sheltered southward-facing aspect at the foot of mountainous headlands, these two harbours remain in my mind as emblems of Ireland's west coast, which can be difficult and even daunting terrain for the cyclist, but which also offers many remarkable and memorable delights.

7
LAKES

Routes 18–22

Route 18:
Lough Derg – Woodford River to Killaloe

OS 15 (Galway, Offaly) and 18 (Tipperary). Distance: approx. 30 miles

Location: Lough Derg, lowest and largest of the Shannon lakes, lies NE of Limerick (and is not to be confused with the lake of the same name in County Donegal); Killaloe, at the lake's foot, is some 10m NE of Limerick city. Woodford is 6m W of the shore a few miles S of the lake's head.

Itinerary: From Woodford, follow the classified road SE until you reach the crossroads, and there turn right on the main road S via Gorteeny and Whitegate to Mountshannon (10m). Keep on the same road to Tuamgraney (19m), where the main route swings W towards Tulla: you must keep left, climbing below Caher Mountain (23m) and running alongside the lake to Killaloe (30m).

Killarney's lakes are famous, and scenic – but a little crowded. Less well-known, just as fine, and virtually deserted are Ireland's numberless other loughs, large and small. Lakes feature in several rides already described (for instance, routes 7 and 8). Donegal, Sligo, Mayo, Leitrim, Cavan, Galway, Roscommon, Longford, Westmeath – in any or all of these counties, the cyclist can find lonely tree-fringed and mountain-backed waters. Often, quiet lanes run for miles alongside them, and it is such delightful rides as these that are highlighted in the present chapter.

Most of the lakes lie north of the Dublin–Galway axis. Apart from the Killarney lakes, the main exception is beautiful Lough Derg, lowest and largest of the broad waters into which the Shannon spreads as it wanders down from Cavan through Leitrim and so, marking the border between counties and the boundary between regions, finds its way across the plain and through Limerick to the sea.

I arrived at Lough Derg after a long ride – too long – from beyond Cong and Clonbur (see routes 7 and 22) and over the plain of south-east County Galway. The last stretch, across bogs and thickets where the Cappagh River flows down through Duniry, was the pleasantest, but by the time I reached the shores of the lake I was aching for rest. As usually happens when you are overtired, I set off in search of a campsite down lane after lane, tempting on the map or promising at their outset, only to find them running into weed-choked thickets or cultivated, enclosed land. This flat stretch of country, just north of where the Woodford River enters Lough Derg, has three lanes shown on the map as running right to the water's edge: two simply stopped amidst tangled, uncampable woods and marshland, while a third, running down to a quay, did culminate in a little grassy clearing – but three cruisers moored alongside had three radios blaring, vying to destroy the evening calm.

All this had an interesting and happy end: my first experience of camping on a bog. Bogs, as I explained in chapter 1, are not the soggy marshes you may imagine. In dry weather such as I had been enjoying for several days, they are firm, springy, sweet-smelling places. There is a tract of raised-bog running up from the north-western shore of Lough Derg, part of it machine-worked by Bord na Mona, and it was on a stretch of this that I put up my tent, with the water of the lake tantalisingly half-seen through woods on the far side of the track which I had followed. This track was edged with burnt gorse: someone had evidently fired the bushes to prevent them getting a hold on the turf, which just here was not being harvested by machine, but stood cut in drying stacks ready to be taken home by local villagers. The half-burnt stalks would make good fuel, although I had to gather a sizeable pile of them. . . . I lit my fire and stretched in the last warmth of the sun. If it was not on the shore of the lake, still this was a fine quiet spot. . . . Then I heard the motor of a car running nearer and nearer down the track towards me.

I felt a flicker of anxiety: what if I were asked what I thought I was doing here, and by what authority I had presumed to light a fire? I need not have worried. The car stopped and a man and his ten-year-old son got out and went to load turf into bags. They came over and talked for a few minutes before the man, apologising for having disturbed the calm of my evening, said goodnight and drove off, having assured me that a small fire was absolutely no danger to the bog.

There was a flurry of misty rain next morning, and in its grey, luminous freshness I contrived to get lost in the lanes south of the Woodford River. Pressing down along narrower and rougher tracks, I came at length to a muddy path which ran in front of a farmhouse: here a flock of geese, who had certainly never before set eyes on a cycle-tourist in flapping yellow cape and loaded with uncouth equipment, burst hissing across my road. A young woman, almost as surprised as the geese, came to the door and returned my embarrassed greeting. I rode a hundred yards further: the path went in at the corner of an unkempt pasture and came to an end in ruts and puddles and tall clumps of thistles. Turning back, I negotiated my way past the geese – again their outcry brought their nonplussed mistress to her door – and picked a route through to the main road at last: this was a poor start to my rather ambitious plan of riding south all the way to Aherlow (see route 3), for I had now spent an hour or more without making perceptible progress in the direction I wished to take.

However, the main road is easily followed, not busy, and increasingly lovely as you ride south. Through the hamlets of Gorteeny and Whitegate – small places with hardly a shop between them – you keep a mile and more from the lough's edge, with glimpses of shining, island-studded water across intervening pastures and woods. After Mountshannon, running to Scarriff with the uplands of Slieve Aughty and Slieve Bernagh to your right, the journey becomes enchanting, and so continues all the way to Killaloe. There is a stiffish climb (the only one in all these thirty miles) after Tuamgraney: now, the Arra Mountains come into view on the far side of the lake, a fine backdrop to its last southern miles. There are fishing piers and boats to hire and an 'official' campsite or two right beside the water: everything for a lakeside holiday, but nothing to damage the underlying sense of calm and solitude.

Route 19:
Lough Ree and Lough Boderg – Glassan to Carrick-on-Carrick

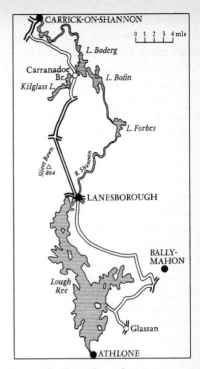

OS 12 (Longford, Roscommon).
Distance: approx. 50 miles

Location: Glassan is 5m NE of Athlone, near the foot of Lough Ree. Lanesborough is at the head of the lough, and Lough Boderg is some 12m due north. Carrick-on-Shannon lies on the river some 8m further to the NW.

Itinerary: From Glassan, take lanes due NW to reach the lakeside on a dead-end road just N of Portlick Castle (3m). From here, follow lanes NE to join the main Athlone–Edgeworthstown classified road just at Tang, where it crosses the river Tang, before forking left on lanes again and so in a long crescent NW to Lanesborough (27m). Take the classified road NNW out of Lanesborough towards Strokestown, crossing the main N5 highway at Scramoge (36m) and forking left 4m beyond this crossroads to cross Lough Boderg at Carranadoe Bridge (43m). From here take lanes NW to join the classified Carrick–Elphin road just outside Carrick-on-Shannon (50m).

For the cyclist, Lough Ree is a frustrating lake, for nowhere on either shore does a lane follow the water's edge for more than a mile or two. There are several dead-end lanes and tracks (more, I suspect, than are shown on the OS map) which run down to the shore, however. Just beyond Glassan, for instance, half a dozen miles north-east of Athlone, small roads take you out along Killinure and Rinardoo bays, or down to the 'Amenity Area' at Portlick. This 'Amenity' really is what it is called, and not a municipal dump, which is what the term generally denotes in my part of the world: Portlick has picnic tables, and beyond them, over a car-proof stile, an accessible stretch of lakeside, with thorn thickets and a beach of grey-yellow limestone rocks and pebbles. You will see thickly wooded islands, misty or clear-cut above bright water as the weather has it, and visited by motor-launches and sailing dinghies: Athlone is a great centre of waterborne tourism. Water-fowl haunt the shores – and so do hunters, whose guns reverberate until dark has fallen among the woods and marshes all around you.

From Portlick, you can find your way (with care) on lanes to the main road that runs north-east through this stretch of Longford – 'Poet's Country', it is often called, in deference to the memory of Oliver Goldsmith, who was born and brought up nearby. The landscape is unspectacular, I suppose, but charming, with great wide skies, and views south, when your road climbs some winding ridge, away across the unbroken pastoral spaces of the central plain. Having found the main road, you turn off it once again, swinging on empty lanes in a wide crescent up towards Lanes-borough at the head of Lough Ree. You pass signs to Elfeet Bay, Barley Harbour, Newtown Cashel: on a sunny morning, and if we had not been looking forward to our breakfast, we would perhaps have ridden down dead-end lanes to one of these lost lakeside hamlets, and gazed across to the island of Inchcleraun where the legendary Queen Maeve is said to have ended her days.

The last few miles before Lanesborough take you across a tract of turf which illustrates as well as any I have seen the aptness of the term 'raised-bog': the bog rose in a plump cushion on either side of us as we rode through mizzling, kindly rain: its colour, a rich and warm contrast to the greens and greys of the landscape around, seemed almost an Impressionist's Provençal brushstroke dashed across some restrained Atlantic watercolour.

Turf is harvested all about Lanesborough, and a power station in the town burns the fuel – and also warms the Shannon, favouring, it is said, the growth of exceptionally large fish (all this

country is beloved of anglers). It surprised us, then, that a leaflet
we browsed through while we ate a good breakfast, a brochure
produced by the local tourist authorities, informed the reader that
turf-bogs are the residue of long-dead trees. They are in fact
formed by accumulating mosses. You may see oaks, pines and
other trees imprisoned, half-petrified, in a stretch of turf: a fine
example is on the western shore of Lough Mask, as you ride up
towards Lough Nafooey from Toormakeady (see route 22). But
such bog-trapped forests are incidental victims of the moss, and
not necessary constituents of turf as fuel.

North-west from Lanesborough, beyond where the Strokestown
road crosses the wide (but almost empty) N5, you come to one of
the loveliest and most secret places of Ireland, the drumlins of
north-east Roscommon. Their smooth, convex slopes topped with a
dark pinewood or chequered into small fields, the drumlins here
compose a hill country of strangely reduced scale, with summits a
hundred or two hundred feet high separated by hollows half a mile
across. The poor drainage of this area – even the mighty Shannon
threads its way with difficulty, through twists and turns and lakes
and pools – favours a marshy flora of restrained and watery
charm, where spikes of wild iris, clumps of rushes, and patches of
pale brown reeds alternate with the grasslands, themselves divided
into a patchwork as dark uncut pastures flank straw-pale fields
where the hay is newly made.

   This drumlin country begins as you drop beyond the far tip of
Slieve Bawn, a striking, narrow ridge visible on a clear day far into
east Mayo and Galway, and marking the point where the level
midland plain gives way to the tangled, complex uplands of the
upper Shannon Valley. Riding obliquely out of Lanesborough
towards the ridge, you will see rough bogs and pastures on its
lower slopes, and extensive afforestation (veiled when we passed
in tongues of billowing mist) towards the top. Almost at the end of
the ridge, you turn off left and drop into the silent valley of Kilglass
Lake. We rode this exquisite waterside road in 'soft rain', which
covered our tracksuits with a dew of tiny beads but was too warm,
too fine, too kind to make us damp. Beyond lost, misty Kilglass
Lake, you are skirting the Shannon – or rather, the southern part of
Lough Boderg, one of the lakes and pools which make up the river
hereabouts. At its narrowest point, this lough is crossed by

Carranadoe Bridge: you can prop your bike against the parapet and climb down to a stretch of neatly-kept grass alongside a stone quay, with rings and bollards for the Shannon cruisers to tie up. The water, at once lake and river, stretches and spreads all round you, but here flows through the bridge's single arch. The distinctive, austere and yet pastoral drumlin landscape contrasts with the slim ridge of Slieve Bawn away to the south. The scene, both times I was there, was lost in an extraordinary peace and silence. For me, this is one of the wonderful places of Ireland, a place which could be found in no other country and which in itself alone would repay all the long journey you have made to come here.

As we drank our second cup of tea, the thinning clouds broke suddenly and afternoon sunlight brightened the green hills and turned the lough's colour in a few minutes from hazy greys to cheerful blues. The bridge, the two boats moored at the quay, and the tussocky lakeside fields were doubled in the reflecting water. The brightness held, and strengthened, as we rode away towards Carrick, at first over narrow and particularly bumpy lanes through the hamlet of Kilmore, and then north-west, still through lovely drumlin country, on smoother surfaces.

Route 20:
Lough Key and Lough Arrow –
Carrick-on-Shannon to Riverstown

OS 7 (Sligo, Leitrim). Distance: approx. 30 miles

Location: For Carrick-on-Shannon, see preceding route. Lough Key lies some 6m NW of Carrick; Lough Arrow is directly above Lough Key. Riverstown is 3m NNW of the head of Lough Arrow, and some 10m SSE of Sligo town.

Itinerary: Leave Carrick on the main road for Drumshanbo, but turn almost immediately left on lanes, crossing the Shannon but keeping E of the Boyle River through Cootehall to Knockvicar Bridge (8m). Ride on lanes as close as possible to the S shore of Lough Key (apart from the short detour to Fin Lough), through the Forest Park and so to Boyle (14m). North out of Boyle on the N4, turn right after 1m on lanes that follow the W shore of Lough Key up to Corrigeenroe (19m), and continue to the E shore of Lough Arrow and so up to Riverstown (30m) above the lake's head.

Lough Key and Lough Arrow, two of the prettiest lakes in Ireland, have for the cyclist the special charm of quiet lanes offering continuous views across the water. Lough Key is perhaps the more celebrated: it was praised by the English agriculturist and traveller, Arthur Young, and for the modern waterborne tourist it has the advantage of forming part of the Boyle River, which flows to join the Shannon just above Carrick. I myself found Lough Arrow (which I first visited in fine cold September weather in 1986) still more charming, with the Bricklieve Mountains to the west making a backdrop for the long headland of Annaghloy House and for the narrow, wooded islands where cows graze, marooned temporarily on waterlocked pastures. Both lakes are finely wooded, and the demesne of Rockingham House, twice burned and still in ruins, has been turned into a public Forest Park which incorporates a spacious, sylvan campsite.

To reach Lough Key from Carrick-on-Shannon, you must leave on the Drumshanbo road, and then take a small lane which runs on northwards where the classified road swings away to the north-east. Here you are briefly in County Leitrim – not far, indeed, from the little village after which the county is called (just as the hamlet of Mayo has given its name to a great expanse of mountain, moor, plain, lake and wild sea-coast).

The lane crosses the Shannon, a narrow waterway just here, although a few miles to the north it broadens again into Lough Allen, highest of the Shannon lakes. You follow the Boyle River, visible across beautiful rushy meadows as a series of broad shining pools. At Cootehall, and again at Knockvicar, these pools dwindle to a bridgeable width, and at Knockvicar you cross the bridge, with a pleasant quay below you where cruisers can tie up. Riding west, you enter the wooded demesne of Rockingham, with Lough Key invisible beyond the trees to your north. A small detour left will bring you to Lough Fin, a small fowl-haunted lake with reedflats and woods on three sides and purple hills rising in the distance beyond. We arrived here on a still, warm evening after a long day's journey up from near Athlone (see route 19), and were delighted to pitch our tent in the strip of grassland between the road and the lake, and to sit drinking white wine on the simple wooden jetty that runs out over the water.

Next morning, we woke to drenching rain – the first of three thoroughly wet days that punctuated the otherwise good weather we enjoyed in August 1987. I succeeded, I cannot imagine how, in lighting a fire and keeping a kettle on the boil for successive cups of tea. Three or four of these gave us heart at last to strike camp and brave the wet: wrapped in capes, sheltered by helmets, we warmed up and even dried out a little as we set off along glistening lanes, spray hissing out from beneath our tyres, feeling as much like mariners as like explorers on dry land (there was no dry land). On such a morning, the Forest Park, some parts of which you must pay to visit, was doing little trade: the disconsolate figure of a ticket-seller in a lonely booth seemed an emblem of the struggle which Irish tourism must wage with the fickle Irish summer.

The town of Boyle lies to the west of the park. This will be the last opportunity you will get to shop until you reach Riverstown, at least – and even there, where we did find a welcoming pub ('the landlord doesn't do coffee,' we were told, 'but he'll do it if you ask': and so it proved), I do not confidently remember seeing a store. Beyond Boyle you must follow the main Sligo road, a busy highway which I would avoid as far as possible: no sooner had we joined it than we saw a stranded truck teetering on the bank beside the road, the driver speaking glumly but collectedly into his cellular telephone.

Turning right along a signposted Scenic Route, you begin a ride, delightful even in misty rain, above the wooded shores and islands of Lough Key. (If pressed for time, you can ride directly from Knockvicar up the east side of the lake, but this longer route gives more, and better, views.) When you reach the crossroads at Corrigeenroe, you must press straight across, heading north-east before turning left to run down to Lough Arrow. When I was there with Kate, we took a wrong turning: it was so wet that we dared hardly take out our soggy map and expose it yet again to the rain. We had cycled three or four miles out of our way before an expatriate Englishman, a Brummie who had been living, he told us, for some years in these parts, put us right. We came across him in trying circumstances: he had been the driver or passenger, we never asked which, of a car which, taking a blind bend too fast on the slippery road, had collided head-on with a tractor. The tractor, naturally, had come off best, but nobody was hurt and our man did not seem much put out. As we turned back for Corrigeenroe and the right road, he told us that there would be a good music session, next Saturday, at John James Regan's. 'Where was that?' we asked. 'In the middle of nowhere,' he told us – anyone would direct us, we need only ask. This, no doubt, was one of the authentic sessions you hear of by word of mouth, and a different thing from the 'traditional Irish muzak' on offer in many hotels and pubs.

We would be in Donegal at the weekend, we said, but thanked him anyway. Riding on, I was struck by the fact that of the three men at the roadside, it had been the expatriate who had struck up a conversation with us: much less cultural difference, even after years in Ireland, between him and us than between ourselves and the other two – both, by the look of them, local farmers. The Englishman wore an earring and had the relaxed air, despite the car crash, of someone schooled in the soft school of the 1960s, from which I too count myself a graduate. I wonder what he did for a living in this remote farming country: 'I'm from Birmingham, but I've lived in these parts for years' – clear enough, from his tone in saying this, that he had no wish or intention of going back.

My memory of Lough Arrow was of the glorious September of

1986. Now, it was as lovely as I recalled, and, like any lake, made the best of what damp brightness there was. But the mountains were lost in mist, and there was no delightful contrast of sparkling water and dark wooded shore. We picnicked, damply, in a sloping field towards the lake's southern end, and then rode through a last hour of rain up past moorings and lakeside bungalows and ruined Ballindoon Castle to the fine prospect back over the water at the lough's head.

I say 'head', assuming that an underground watercourse links Lough Arrow with Lough Key below it, and so by the Boyle River to the Shannon. If my assumption is correct, then the stream which enters the lake here, and which the lane follows up towards Riverstown, empties its waters at length into the Shannon estuary below far-off Limerick. At Riverstown, you meet with streams that flow the other, shorter way to Sligo, or rather to Ballysodare Bay five miles south of Sligo. Marking as it thus might the drainage limit of the great Shannon, Riverstown would merit its watery name in this fine, drumlin-strewn, watery country. Riverstown, 'Baile Idir Dha Abhann', the town between the two rivers. Abhann is the Irish form of Afon or Avon, that much-encountered river-name which is one of the Celtic traces left in our Welsh and English maps.

Route 21:
Lough Melvin and Lough Gill – Ballyshannon to the Lake Isle of Innisfree

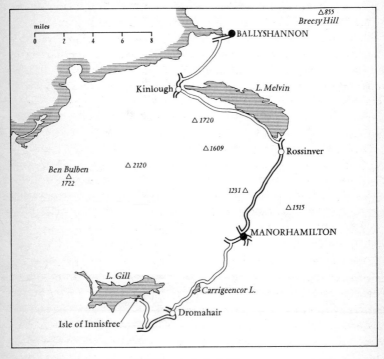

OS 3 (South Donegal) and 7 (Sligo, Leitrim). Distance: approx. 35 miles

Location: Lough Melvin lies on the Border between County Leitrim and County Fermanagh (Northern Ireland), about 15m NW of Sligo town. Lough Gill is immediately E of Sligo.

Itinerary: Leaving Ballyshannon on the main Bundoran and Sligo road, shortly out of town take a lane left to Kinlough, where you follow the classified road for about 1m before turning on a lane left along the S shore of Lough Melvin to Rossinver (16m). Stay on the classified road, which you must take right at the foot of the lake, over into Manorhamilton (23m). Leave Manorhamilton on the main Sligo road, turn left on lanes immediately after crossing the Bonet River, and so on lanes, keeping above Carrigeencor Lake, SW to Dromahair (30m). From Dromahair take the more southerly of two classified roads signposted to Sligo, turning off this about 3m out of town down a lane, right, signposted to Lake Isle of Innisfree (35m).

Lough Gill – where this route ends – is visited by literary tourists, for here you will find Yeats' Lake Isle of Innisfree. The poem named for the island is early, drowsy Yeats, an anthology piece which hardly represents his strongest gifts. As for the island, and the lake, they are charming: but to anyone who knows the sterner and remoter lakes of Mayo, Lough Gill will seem a distinctly amenable place of exile: the saints and scholars who once chose such retreats as the bare Skellig rocks west of the Iveragh Peninsula would certainly have found Innisfree, two minutes from the lane's end by rowing-boat, unsuitably accessible.

Lough Melvin – a long, sickle-shaped lake backed to the south by the Dartry Mountains – is unfrequented. The Northern Ireland border runs across its eastern waters, and the B53/L16, between Garrison (at the lake's head) in Fermanagh and Manorhamilton in Leitrim, is an 'unapproved road', with no control point at the frontier, and accordingly barred to traffic. Lough Melvin is visited only by those who go out of their way to see it, and travel south out of Donegal by way of these empty roads rather than through Sligo or on the more direct route from Kinlough to Manorhamilton past Glenade Lough in the heart of the Dartry massif.

Ballyshannon (see routes 9 and 10) is a bustling town, with the main Sligo–Donegal road running through it, and with a turning off to Enniskillen via the Belleek frontier post. It is a good place to shop (as is Manorhamilton further on): if you chose to spend a few hours there, you would no doubt find a way down onto the spreading sands of its estuary where the waters of the complex Erne river system, dammed for hydroelectric power in Assaroe Lake (the dam looms over Ballyshannon), eventually find their way to the sea.

Leaving Ballyshannon on the main Sligo road, you turn off just out of town on a lane to Kinlough, an uneventful, flattish stretch relieved by the Dartry massif on the skyline and by the pretty, tree-fringed Drowse River. You cross this on a bridge with an inscription to the Four Masters, seventeenth-century clerics who compiled an early written history of Ireland. These 'Annals of the Four Masters' were written, the inscription claims, at nearby

Rossfriar Abbey, on the north shore of Lough Melvin; they are also said to have been compiled at the Franciscan monastery (now in ruins) at Donegal, and a monument to the Four Masters, as well as a church dedicated to them, will be found in Donegal town.

At Kinlough you come to another classified road, and then turn off to the left just as you leave the village. The first few miles of this lane will give you occasional glimpses of Lough Melvin – although you could leave your bike in the hedge and walk down any of the several footpaths marked 'Fishing/Iascareacht' (I hope I have got the Irish spelling right; I am relying on my memory). Where the lane does eventually run down alongside the water, there is more elaborate provision for anglers, the simple, whitewashed Breffni lodge, with jetties for the launching of those flat-bottomed rowing-boats you will see on so many Irish lakes. We picnicked on the pier in hot sun, and watched a family of anglers, unsuccessful so far that day, put ashore to eat their own lunch: the two boys seemed less interested in food than in continuing to fish from the jetty.

The lane continues near the lakeshore for four miles or so. The steep-sided Dartry Mountains to your right contrast pleasantly with views across the lake to the islands and wooded headlands of Fermanagh, and beyond them to the moors and hills of the Pullans (see route 10), with Breesy Hill prominent. At the head of the lake, where you turn right on the classified road, a signpost points down a track to the ruined medieval church of Rossinver. South-east of here is a more substantial relic of the past, the Worm Ditch, which legend regards as the trace left by the slitherings of a giant snake, but which is probably, like Offa's Dyke, an old frontier earthwork: traces of it remain from Newry in the east to Bundoran in the west. It marked the boundary of the old province of Ulster, and the modern Border runs by here too. You are no more than a mile or two from it as you join the classified road. It is ironic that nearby Kiltyclogher was the birthplace of Sean MacDiarmada, one of the signatories of the Proclamation of the Irish Republic issued at Easter 1916. MacDiarmada, with all the other signatories, was shot by the British following the defeat of the Easter Rising. A statue commemorates him at Kiltyclogher.

These bitter associations can hardly be avoided as you ride over towards Manorhamilton, for the road is eerily empty, palpably blighted by its truncation at the Border. You pass a forlorn petrol station, which was up for sale when we were there – in the hands of an auctioneer in far-off Navan, in County Meath, where potential buyers might not realise that the property stands in so uncommercial a location. Further on, there is a collapsed church, with no signboard even to show what saint it is dedicated to, not an architecturally distinguished ruin but a mere dilapidated pile, its roof half fallen in.

Scenically, this long (and mostly gentle) climb is glorious riding, both for the green valley near at hand and for the long views back: make sure to pause and enjoy a last prospect towards the south Donegal mountains. Towards the col, upwards of 600 feet, I stopped to talk with a farmer lifting potatoes from the plot around his house. They were not ready yet, he said – he had just lifted a handful to see how they were getting on: but with a few fine days, they would be doing well. It was sunny as we talked, but he feared that it would 'teem with rain' later, and the prospect into Leitrim, as we began the long descent southwards, was memorably stormy, with black and yellow clouds piled above the bare uplands about Lough Allen to the east. Manorhamilton, an attractive, slaty town in the valley of the river Bonet, glistened in thundery light, but we shopped optimistically, with a view to camping out that night. Our optimism proved well-founded, for we had no more than a few showery drops, although away inland heavy veils of rain swung across the sides of mountains and blurred the valleys.

We bought vegetables in a shop that might have been found in Bath or Brighton, a co-op selling wholefoods and local organic produce, as well as Nicaraguan coffee, but – a notice expressly stated – no South African produce. In this outpost of the Irish green movement, we bought the current issue of *North-West Newsletter*, incorporating the journal of the Irish organic farmers' association. The paper, 'celebrating a decade of Irish rural alternatives', had articles on aromatherapy, farmhouse cheesemaking, and coping with wet weather, as well as an interview with Matthias Kreuzeder, an organic farmer and West German Green MP. I do not know how far this shop was integrated with the local farming economy: the woman who served us had just been away, she told us, for a week in Dublin, and this led me (perhaps wrongly) to assume that the co-op had been set up, here in remote Leitrim, by voluntary exiles from the metropolis. Here as in Britain, the green movement struggles to express, and realise, a vision of the future not dependent on short-term, market-based and unsustainable notions of 'success'. It is all the harder to win support for such a vision in a country still poor by EEC standards, and where the pressure for jobs of whatever kind is intense, especially in the countryside. The *Newsletter* was my first introduction to this part of Ireland's alternative culture, and I was pleased to read it, even though I could not feel enthusiastic about the recipe for Pea Pod Wine on page 10.

Beyond Manorhamilton comes more fine cycling, first in bogs and pastures of the broadening Bonet valley, and then in exquisite marshy drumlin country between Carrigeencor Lake and Droma-hair. Dromahair is an attractive, spaciously laid out village, with two contrasting church spires, one modest and whitewashed, the other slate-roofed and impressive. Here too, on the bank of the Bonet, are ruins of a sixteenth-century Franciscan abbey. However, I shall remember Dromahair less for these Christian buildings than for the pagan meaning of its delightful Irish name, 'Druim dha Eithiar', translated by Sean Jennett as 'the ridge of the two air demons'. This seems to me a name evocative of lovers' airy, demonic quarrels: as Donne writes (in *A Nocturnal Upon St Lucie's Day*),

> Oft a flood
> Have we two wept, and so
> Drown'd the whole world, us two; oft did we grow
> To be two Chaoses . . .

More prosaically, you may note that Drom- and Drum- are frequent place-name elements all around here: Drumshanbo, Drumsna, 'Cora Droma Ruisc' (Carrick-on-Shannon) are exam-ples. I have explained that the Irish diminutive form, anglicised as 'drumlin', has passed into general use as a geological term.

From Dromahair, it is three miles or so to the turning for Innisfree: make sure to follow the more southerly of the two classified roads both, confusingly, signposted to Sligo. The turning for Lough Gill and Innisfree runs down through lovely meadows beside the Bonet, and is clearly marked for the benefit of passing Yeatsians. You will be pleasantly surprised if you are fearing some commercial despoliation of the lakeside: there is an unobtrusive teashop and a notice telling you where you can hire boats to row the hundred yards to the Isle, but nothing detracts from the quiet charm of the lough, with its prospect over gleaming water and across lower, tangled hills to the Ben Bulben range.

Route 22:
Lough Mask and Lough Nafooey

OS 11 (South Mayo). Distance: approx. 32 miles

Location: Lough Mask separates the Mayo plain from the Connemara Mountains. Partry, at the lough's head, is 11m due S of Castlebar; Clonbur, at its foot, is on the isthmus between Loughs Mask and Corrib. The route terminates on the E shore of the lake about 4m SW of Ballinrobe.

Itinerary: From Partry, on the main Castlebar–Galway road, take the road right and fork left after less than 1m to Srah hamlet (3m). Turn left and ride S along the shore of the lake through Toormakeady (6m) and, keeping at the water's edge as long as possible, climb eventually to Lough Nafooey (16m). On reaching the foot of Lough Nafooey, double back left and follow the Finny River down to Ferry Bridge (21m). Continue on lanes to Clonbur and on the classified road to Cong (28m). Turn left on a lane, cross the canal, and turn immediately left again, and follow lanes to the dead end at Inishcong, where the OS map shows the ruins of a castle and an abbey (32m).

Ireland, as we have seen, has many lakes that offer views across the water to near or distant mountains. Beside almost every one of them, you will enjoy a solitude and silence all but unimaginable in crowded England. How many memorable evenings I have spent on the shores of Mayo lakes: beside Lough Feeagh (route 8) looking north-west to the Nephin Beg range, on the wood-fringed rock-strewn strand of Lough Cullin (route 11) below Ben Nephin, and on both east and west shores of beautiful Lough Mask, a lake I have visited four times and which I can see, now, when I shut my eyes. On the west shore, where the Finny River flows through sandy grass-banks and gorse-thickets to join the stretch of water running west from Ferry Bridge, I have camped, alone and with Kate, beneath the superb mountain amphitheatre. On the flat east shore, where the Mayo plains roll away behind you and where close-bitten sheep-pastures lie among hedges of thorn and clumps of rowan and dry stone walls, we have sat by our fire, surrounded by great blocks of rain-pitted honey-coloured limestone, and

looked over the lake to the unbroken arc of mountains: Croagh
Patrick away to the north, the long level Partry ridge, and closer at
hand the steep sides of Maumtrasna, licked perhaps by swirling
tongues of mist and cloud, or rising blue and tranquil into the
Connemara sky.

Riding west and then south from Partry, you soon reach the shore
of Lough Mask, and its waters remain in view for most of the ten
miles you ride down its western ridge. There are houses and small
farms on the slopes above you, but the land between road and
lakeside is for the most part unfenced and undeveloped. The only
settlement of any size is Toormakeady, a Gaeltacht village with
crafts and a college and a row of attractive modern holiday
cottages. You might happily ride for a whole day beside the water:
this route, to judge by the many Continental cyclists we saw when
we were last there, has become celebrated (perhaps by word of
mouth), and indeed a glance at the map tells you that here you will
find cycling which is at once easy, quiet and gloriously scenic.

Some miles south of Toormakeady you climb towards the
mountains. Passing between two small peaks, and rising to around
400 feet, the road soon drops again to the foot of Lough Nafooey
(see route 7): a cow, maybe, is grazing in rough pasture beside the
bright sandy beaches at one end or another of the lake. You follow
the slow, deep Finny River down to Lough Mask again, passing,
very probably, a fisherman wading in tall boots along this most
beautiful stretch of water. Beyond the arm of the lake, running up
towards the 2,000-foot slopes which cradle it, farms cling to the
narrow shoreline, their sheep-grazing marked out by stone walls
on the rough, steep moors above.

At Ferry Bridge, the first time we came this way, we stopped: the
parapet sheltered our stove while we made coffee, and the views in
every direction made us stay for another cup. Then comes the run
into Clonbur, with thickets blocking the view over the lake, but
when you do get a clear prospect northwards its waters stretch
with vivid brightness away towards Castlebar and the dark hills
behind it. Beyond Clonbur (where you can buy basic food) and
Cong, you turn off left beside the ill-fated canal, which was built to
link Lough Mask to Lough Corrib just a couple of miles south, but
which, being dug in porous limestone, held no water.

Navigating carefully through the lanes, you should be able to find your way down to the shore at Inishcong (also called Inishmaine). If you have time, leave your bicycle at the ford which links the island to the shore and walk out westwards: by climbing onto west-facing slopes, you can gain a particularly fine view over towards the far side of the lake. As you walk back, you will see, lost and grey and ruinous among fine woods, Loughmask House, once the home of the famous (or notorious) Captain Boycott. A more obscure and more cheering relic of the nineteenth century is the work of two retired naval officers – their names long ago escaped my memory – who patiently sounded the depths and shallows of Lough Mask: the chart they made hangs, or anyway used to hang, in a bank in Headford. It has no practical value: the lough must surely be deep enough everywhere but at the shoreline for the flat-bottomed clinker-built craft which are the only kind you will see afloat there, and if such craft do touch a shoal, I suppose they come to little harm. However, the chart's justification need not lie in whatever use it may or may not have: what enchanted hours the two officers must have passed, surveying the lake to draw it.

Twice now I have woken on the shore near Inishmaine to the last dawn of an Irish holiday. Riding east to the station at Roscommon or Castlerea, you can look back – as Kate and I looked back – but you will see nothing of the low-lying lake. However, the mountains beyond stay within view for miles, rising into the horizon as you climb a ridge and dropping out of sight again as your road descends. Time after time, on a clear day, you may think you have seen the last of them – the last of Croagh Patrick, too, and of Ben Nephin – only to catch your breath as they appear, remote now and pale against the still paler sky, in yet one more prospect west. In the end, somewhere in the rolling limestone south-east of Claremorris, you must accept that they really have gone, now – not for good, but until you come back to Ireland, and ride once more towards them.

Index